CAMBRIDGE LIBRARY COLLECTION

Books of enduring scholarly value

Archaeology

The discovery of material remains from the recent or the ancient past has always been a source of fascination, but the development of archaeology as an academic discipline which interpreted such finds is relatively recent. It was the work of Winckelmann at Pompeii in the 1760s which first revealed the potential of systematic excavation to scholars and the wider public. Pioneering figures of the nineteenth century such as Schliemann, Layard and Petrie transformed archaeology from a search for ancient artifacts, by means as crude as using gunpowder to break into a tomb, to a science which drew from a wide range of disciplines - ancient languages and literature, geology, chemistry, social history - to increase our understanding of human life and society in the remote past.

Cretan Pictographs and Prae-Phoenician Script

Sir Arthur John Evans (1851–1941) famously excavated the ruins of Knossos on Crete and uncovered the remains of its Bronze Age Minoan civilisation (as described in his multi-volume work *The Palace of Minos at Knossos*, also reissued in this series). But he had already visited the island prior to this: in 1894, during his first trip, he found examples of an ancient pictographic writing system that pre-dated the Phoenician alphabet later adapted by the Greeks. First published in 1895, this work, illustrated with examples throughout, documents and describes these discoveries, and demonstrates that the earliest finds date from a period before even the most ancient known Semitic scripts. Evans also records evidence of later scripts which were subsequently categorised as Linear A and Linear B (only the latter has been deciphered since his death). The final section of the book describes in detail the pottery and other finds from the Hagios Onuphrios deposit.

Cambridge University Press has long been a pioneer in the reissuing of out-of-print titles from its own backlist, producing digital reprints of books that are still sought after by scholars and students but could not be reprinted economically using traditional technology. The Cambridge Library Collection extends this activity to a wider range of books which are still of importance to researchers and professionals, either for the source material they contain, or as landmarks in the history of their academic discipline.

Drawing from the world-renowned collections in the Cambridge University Library and other partner libraries, and guided by the advice of experts in each subject area, Cambridge University Press is using state-of-the-art scanning machines in its own Printing House to capture the content of each book selected for inclusion. The files are processed to give a consistently clear, crisp image, and the books finished to the high quality standard for which the Press is recognised around the world. The latest print-on-demand technology ensures that the books will remain available indefinitely, and that orders for single or multiple copies can quickly be supplied.

The Cambridge Library Collection brings back to life books of enduring scholarly value (including out-of-copyright works originally issued by other publishers) across a wide range of disciplines in the humanities and social sciences and in science and technology.

Cretan Pictographs
and
Prae-Phoenician Script

*With an Account of a Sepulchral Deposit
at Hagios Onuphrios near Phaestos
in Its Relation to Primitive Cretan
and Aegean Culture*

Arthur John Evans

CAMBRIDGE
UNIVERSITY PRESS

CAMBRIDGE UNIVERSITY PRESS

Cambridge, New York, Melbourne, Madrid, Cape Town,
Singapore, São Paolo, Delhi, Mexico City

Published in the United States of America by Cambridge University Press, New York

www.cambridge.org
Information on this title: www.cambridge.org/9781108060974

© in this compilation Cambridge University Press 2013

This edition first published 1895
This digitally printed version 2013

ISBN 978-1-108-06097-4 Paperback

CRETAN PICTOGRAPHS

AND

PRAE-PHOENICIAN SCRIPT

WITH AN ACCOUNT OF A SEPULCHRAL DEPOSIT
AT HAGIOS ONUPHRIOS NEAR PHAESTOS
IN ITS RELATION TO PRIMITIVE CRETAN
AND AEGEAN CULTURE

BY

ARTHUR J. EVANS, M.A., F.S.A.

KEEPER OF THE ASHMOLEAN MUSEUM
AND HON. FELLOW OF BRASENOSE COLLEGE, OXFORD

WITH A COLOURED PLATE, TABLES, AND 139 ILLUSTRATIONS IN THE TEXT

London
BERNARD QUARITCH, 15 PICCADILLY
New York
G. P. PUTNAM'S SONS, 27 WEST 23D STREET
1895

RICHARD CLAY AND SONS, LIMITED,
LONDON AND BUNGAY.

NOTE.

THE first of these papers is reprinted, by permission, from the *Hellenic Journal* (Vol. xiv. Pt. II. 1895) with some slight additions and corrections. The account of the Hagios Onuphrios deposit and its bearings on the prehistoric culture of the Aegean world is now issued for the first time. Already in 1893, on the occasion of my paper on 'A Mycenaean Treasure from Aegina' I ventured to announce to the Hellenic Society that I had found what I believed to be a clue to the existence of a system of picture-writing in the Greek lands. The result of my explorations in Crete during the spring of 1894 was not only to confirm this discovery as regards the 'pictographic' system but to add distinct evidence of the existence in the island at a very early period of a linear system of writing standing in a certain relation to the pictorial. A summary report of the results of my researches in Crete in the spring of 1894 was sent by me to the *Athenaeum* from Candia on April 25 of last year, and appeared in that Journal on June 23. The *Times* of Aug. 29 published a further account of my Cretan discoveries, written by me at the request of the Editor, and I also read a paper on the subject in the Anthropological Section of the British Association, of which reports appeared in the *Academy* and other papers. On that occasion I called attention for the first time to certain archaeological evidence connecting the Philistines with Mycenaean Crete. In the second paper of this book and the supplement are incorporated some further materials obtained by me during another Cretan journey undertaken this spring.

SUMMARY OF CONTENTS.

ILLUSTRATIONS.

PRIMITIVE PICTOGRAPHS ETC.

THE HAGIOS ONUPHRIOS DEPOSIT, ETC.

PRIMITIVE PICTOGRAPHS
AND A PRAE-PHOENICIAN SCRIPT, FROM CRETE AND THE PELOPONNESE.

PRIMITIVE PICTOGRAPHS AND A PRAE-PHOENICIAN SCRIPT FROM CRETE AND THE PELOPONNESE.

§ I.—Cretan Discoveries.

In the absence of abiding monuments the fact has too generally been lost sight of, that throughout what is now the civilized European area there must once have existed systems of picture-writing such as still survive among the more primitive races of mankind. To find such 'pictographs' in actual use —the term is used in its most comprehensive sense to cover carvings on rocks or other materials whether or not actually overlaid with colour—we must now go further afield. Traces of such may indeed be seen on the rude engravings of some megalithic monuments like that of Gavr Innis, on the rock carvings of Denmark, or the mysterious figures known as the *Maraviglie* wrought on a limestone cliff in the heart of the Maritime Alps, to which may be added others quite recently discovered in the same region.

In Lapland, where designs of this character ornamented the troll-drums of the magicians till within a recent period, survivals of some of the traditional forms may still be found to the present day, engraved on the bowls of their reindeer-horn spoons. Of actual rock-paintings perfectly analogous to those of Cherokees or Zulus, I have myself observed an example—consisting of animals and swastika-like figures painted probably by early Slavonic hands on the face of a rock overhanging a sacred grotto in a fiord of the Bocche di Cattaro.

But the perishable nature of the materials on which picture-writing, having for most part only a temporary value, was usually wrought has been fatal to the survival of primitive European pictographs on any large scale. If we had before us the articles of bark and hide and wood of early man in this quarter of the globe or could still see the tattoo marks on his skin we should have a very different idea of the part once played by picture-writing on European soil. As it is, it is right that the imagination should supply the deficiency of existing evidence.

In the areas embraced by the older civilizations such as Egypt, Babylonia and China, a different kind of influence has been at work, by which the void caused by the disappearance of the more primitive materials may in a great measure be filled up. For there the early pictographic elements, such as we still find them among savage races, were, in the hands of priestly and official castes, developed into a more complicated and exact system of writing, by which however we are enabled in many cases to trace back the original forms of the object selected. The same development from the simple pictographic to the hieroglyphic or quasi-alphabetic stage might naturally have been expected to have taken place in more than one European area had it not been cut short by the invasion of the fully equipped Phoenician system of writing.

Even as it is however, it must be allowed that there are strong *a priori* reasons for believing that in the Greek lands where civilization put forth its earliest blossoms on European soil, some such parallel evolution in the art of writing must have been in the course of working itself out.

For we now know that in the South-Eastern part of our Continent there existed long before the days of direct Phoenician contact an independent form of culture which already as early as the first half of the second millennium before our era might be regarded as in many respects the equal contemporary of those of Egypt and Babylonia. In view of the extraordinary degree of artistic and mechanical development reached by the representatives of what is now conveniently known as the Mycenaean civilization—at least as early, approximately speaking, as the seventeenth century, B.C.—and the wide ramifications of their commerce, is it conceivable, it may be asked, that in the essential matter of writing they were so far behind their rivals on the Southern and Eastern shores of the Mediterranean?

There is moreover a further consideration which tends to make the absence of any system of writing among the Mycenaean peoples still more improbable. At the dawn of history Asia Minor, whether we regard the predominant elements of its population from the point of view of race or of culture, may be said to belong to Europe. Its area from the earliest times of which we have any record was largely in the occupation of the great Thraco-Phrygian race and its offshoots. Its prehistoric remains, as far as we know them from Cyprus to the Troad, fit on to those of a large archaeological area, the continuation of which may be traced over the island stepping-stones of the Aegean to the mainland of Greece, while in the other direction kindred forms extend along the Danubian system to reappear amongst the pile-dwellings of Switzerland and Carniola, the *terre-mare* of the Po valley and even in Ligurian caves. But it is on the Eastern borders of this wide field of primitive culture that recent researches have brought to light the principal seats of the higher form of early civilization conveniently known as Hittite. Living in the Syrian and Cappadocian regions in the immediate proximity of upper Mesopotamia, and almost in the highways as it were of old Chaldean culture, its representatives yet show independent characteristics and traditions, the sources of which seem to be drawn from the North or West. And of these one of the most noteworthy is the possession of an original system of hieroglyphic writing, the relics of which are scattered from the banks of the Orontes to the Western shores of Anatolia. At a later date again we find the Greeks of Cyprus and the inhabitants of a large tract of Asia Minor in the possession of syllabic scripts altogether distinct from the Phoenician alphabet.

When it is once realized how largely the early civilization of the Aegean Islands and even the mainland of Greece was evolved out of similar elements to those of Asia Minor, it must certainly seem surprising that on this side no system of writing belonging to prae-Phoenician times should as yet have been clearly ascertained. The geographical contiguity to Anatolia, and the early trade relations which can be shown to have existed between the Aegean Islands and the valley of the Nile would assuredly, it might be thought, have given an impulse to the higher development of whatever primitive form of picture-writing was already to be found amongst the inhabitants of this Mediterranean region. It is impossible indeed to suppose that this European population was so far below even the Red Indian stage of culture as not to have largely resorted to pictography as an aid to memory and communication. And—even if an existing system was not perfected under the influence of foreign example—the race which laid the arts of Egypt and Western Asia under such heavy contribution was at least capable of borrowing and adapting a system of writing.

It is true that Schliemann's great discoveries at Mycenae produced nothing that could be safely interpreted as a form of script. The objects seen in the field of many of the ordinary Mycenaean gems — the so-called 'island-stones'—are simply inserted as the space left by the principal design suggests, and are primarily of a decorative character—and due to the *horror vacui* of primitive art. Nevertheless, especially when we see a part standing for a whole—as a branch for a tree or the head of an animal for the animal itself—it may be fairly said that many of these gems do bear the impress of people familiar with the expedients of primitive picture-writing, such as we find it still in so many parts of the world. The lentoid and amygdaloid gems in question did not, as we now know, serve the purpose of seals, but were simply ornamental beads worn round the wrist or neck.[1] Like the oriental periapts, however, worn in the same manner at the present day, they may often have been intended to serve as amulets or talismans; and both the principal type of the intaglio and the smaller or abbreviated forms introduced into the field may have possessed something beyond a mere artistic significance. Still more is this likely to have been implied in the case of the engraved designs on the besils of the gold rings from the Mycenaean graves which seem actually to have served the purpose of signets. It certainly is not unreasonable to suppose that in this case some of the smaller objects in the field may have had a conventional religious meaning, and that they were in fact ideographs taken from a recognized hieroglyphic code. The bulls' heads and lions' scalps, the ears of corn and double

---

[1] See Tsountas, Ἀνασκαφαὶ τάφων ἐν Μυκή- ναις. Ἐφ. Ἀρχ. 1888, p. 175. There are probably, as will be seen below, some exceptions to this rule in case of some Cretan lentoid gems presenting groups of symbolic figures.

axe certainly suggest that we have here to deal with symbols of divinity, perhaps standing for the divinity itself, or ideas of cult and sacrifice,—the latter form of symbolism being well brought out by the gold ornaments representing oxes' heads with a double axe between the horns. In the same way, to take an example from the practice of modern savages, a drawing of eyes and beak stood among the Iroquois for the Thunder-Bird or a rayed head for a Spirit among the Ojibwas. The whole of later Greek symbolism may in fact be regarded as a survival, maintained by religious conservatism, from a wide field of primitive pictography. The figure that stands as the personal badge of the names of individuals at times actually appears as the equivalent of the written form of the name, as when a monetary magistrate called Leôn places a *lion* on his dies. The same symbolic script is frequent in the rendering of city names, one of the most interesting examples being found on a coin of Mesembria where the part of the civic legend signifying day is supplied by a *swastika*—the emblem of the midday sun.[2]

The symbols on the Mycenaean seals are themselves of too isolated occurrence to be used straight away as examples of a hieroglyphic system— though there seem to me to be good reasons for supposing that some at least among them did fit on to such a system. But more recently one or two objects have been found at Mycenae itself and in Mycenaean deposits else-where which are calculated more effectually to shake some of the preconceived notions of archaeologists as to the non-existence in Greece of a prae-Phoenician system of writing. The most important of these are the handle of a stone vase apparently of a local material (Fig. 1) found at Mycenae, which has

FIG. 1.—SIGNS ON VASE-HANDLE, MYCENAE.

four, or perhaps five, signs engraved upon it, and the handle of a clay amphora from a chambered tomb in the lower town of Mycenae with three

FIG. 2.—SIGNS ON AMPHORA-HANDLE, MYCENAE.

characters (Fig. 2). Single signs have also been noticed on the handles of two amphoras of the same form as the last found in the Tholos tomb of

---

[2] P. Gardner, *Num. Chron.* 1880, p. 59 ; Head, *Hist. Num.* 237.

Menidi,[3] on a three-handled vase from Nauplia[4] and a stone pestle from
Mycenae.[5]   Dr. Tsountas in describing these finds lays stress on their
occurrence in two cases in groups of three and four respectively, and reasonably asks whether we have not here to deal with some form of writing.
Professor Petrie again has discovered a series of isolated symbols on what he
considers to have been fragments of early Aegean pottery discovered by him
at Gurob in a deposit which he assigns to the period of the Twelfth Dynasty,
and again at Kahun amongst Eighteenth Dynasty relics.[6]

Notwithstanding these indications, however, the last writer on the
Mycenaean and early Aegean culture, M. Perrot, sums up the evidence as
follows : 'The first characteristic which attracts the historian's notice when
he tries to define the prae-Homeric civilization is that it is a stranger to the
use of writing. It knows neither the ideographic signs possessed by Egypt
and Chaldaea nor the alphabet properly so called which Greece was afterwards
to borrow from Phoenicia.' He admits indeed that some of the marks
recently observed on the vase-handles bear resemblance to letters, either
Greek or Cypriote, but observes that they do not seem to form words, and
that they are perhaps nothing more than the marks of the potter or the
proprietor, or ignorant copies of Phoenician or Asianic characters. 'As at
present advised,' he concludes, 'we can continue to affirm that for the whole
of this period, nowhere, neither in the Peloponnese nor in Greece proper, no
more on the buildings than on the thousand objects of luxury or domestic use
that have come out of the tombs, has there anything been discovered which
resembles any kind of writing.'[7]

The evidence which I am now able to bring forward will, I venture to
think, conclusively demonstrate that as a matter of fact an elaborate system
of writing did exist within the limits of the Mycenaean world, and moreover
that two distinct phases of this art are traceable among its population. The
one is pictographic in character like Egyptian hieroglyphics, the other linear
and quasi-alphabetic, much resembling the Cypriote and Asianic syllabaries.

In the course of a visit to Greece in the spring of 1893 I came across
some small three- and four-sided stones perforated along their axis, upon which
had been engraved a series of remarkable symbols. The symbols occurred
in groups on the facets of the stones, and it struck me at once that they
belonged to a hieroglyphic system. They were however quite distinct from

---

[3] Tsountas, Μηκῆναι p. 213. One has a sign
resembling the Greek Π, the other, ⧥ the
Cypriote, pa, ba, or pha.

[4] Ἀρχαιολογικὸν Δελτίον, 1892, p. 73. It
was discovered by Dr. Stais in a tomb of the
Pronoea. On each handle was engraved a sign
like the Greek H but with offshoots from the
top of the upright strokes.

[5] Πρακτικὰ τῆς Ἀρχαιολογικῆς Ἑταιρίας, 1889,
p. 19.   [6] See below, p. 348.

[7] Perrot et Chipiez, La Grèce primitive : l'Art
Mycénien, p. 985. In describing the Knôsian

marks (see below, p. 282) M. Perrot had previously admitted (op. cit. 461) that the Cypriote
signs may have had an Aegean extension 'during
a certain time.' But the subsequent passage on
p. 985 retracts this admission as far as the Mycenaean period is concerned. Dr. Reichel suggests (Homerische Waffen, p. 142) that the
linear designs below the combatants on the silver
fragment from Mycenae (Ἐφ. Ἀρχ. 1891, Pl.
II. 2) are signs of an unknown script. But the
figures in question represent throwing-sticks
(J.H.S. xiii. (1892-3), p. 199, n. 11ᵃ).

Egyptian in character, and though they seemed to show a nearer approach to Hittite forms it was evident that they belonged to an independent series. My inquiries succeeded in tracing these to a Cretan source. Knowing of the considerable collection of 'island' and other early gems in the Museum of Berlin, I addressed myself to Dr. Furtwängler, mentioning my discovery and asking whether any specimens of the forms and characters indicated existed in the Imperial Museum. In response to my inquiries Dr. Furtwängler very courteously sent me several impressions from similarly formed stones in the Berlin Museum, presenting symbols which fitted on to and supplemented the series that I had already obtained. In this case too the source of the stones, as far as it was known, turned out again to be Crete. The impression of a gem taken at Athens some years since by Professor Sayce and kindly placed by him at my disposal supplied a new piece of evidence, and I found that an unclassed four-sided stone in the Ashmolean Museum, which had been brought back by Mr. Greville Chester from Greece, noted by him as having been found at Sparta but really from Crete,[7b] was engraved with symbols belonging to the same series as the others.

The evidence as a whole however clearly pointed to Crete as the principal source of these hieroglyphic forms, and I therefore determined to follow up my investigations on Cretan soil. Landing at Candia early in March 1894, I made my way round the whole centre and East of the island,— including the mountainous districts of Ida and Dikta, the extensive central plain of Messarà and the sites of over twenty ancient cities. The number of relics illustrative of the prehistoric periods of Cretan culture that I was thus able to collect was surprisingly great, and in particular the evidence daily accumulated itself of the very important part played by the Mycenaean form of civilization in Cretan story. And, in what regarded the more special object of my quest, my researches were well rewarded by the discovery *in situ* of traces of a prae-Phoenician system of writing in the island, of which two distinct phases were perceptible, one pictorial and hieroglyphic, the other linear and quasi-alphabetic.

From indications obtained at Candia I was led more particularly to investigate the Eastern part of the island and the land which to the borders of the historic period was still occupied by the Eteocretes or indigenous Cretan stock. Here by the site of Praesos, their principal city, has been discovered a remarkable inscription,[8] which, though written in archaic Greek characters, belongs to an unknown language which we may reasonably regard as the original speech of the Cretan natives before the days of the Greek colonization. This fact by itself renders investigations into the antiquities of this easternmost district of special ethnographic value, and here too may some day be discovered the remains of the shrine of the Diktaean Zeus, mentioned by Strabo as existing in the territory of Praesos.

At Praesos itself, which lies on a conical limestone hill near the modern village of Vavéles I observed, besides its primitive walls of rude horizontal

---

[7b] See below, p. 136.   [8] See below, pp. 354, 355.

and polygonal masonry, fragments of very early pottery, some of which must be classed with the ceramic relics of the first prehistoric city of Hissarlik, while others belonged to the Mycenaean style. I further obtained from a peasant on the spot a prism-shaped stone of the kind of which I was in search, presenting engraved characters (see below, Fig. 29), and subsequently from the same district three other three- and four-sided stones with linear and hieroglyphic symbols (see below, Figs. 22, 26, 38). On the site called Palaekastro, the akropolis of which lies on the easternmost cove of the island, opposite the islet of Grandes, and which represents another ancient city, perhaps Grammion, that was situate between the territories of Praesos and Itanos in the same Eteocretan region, I secured another four-sided stone (see below, Fig. 35), presenting no less than fifteen hieroglyphic symbols. Two other stones of the same pictographic class found in Eastern Crete (see below, Figs. 23, 24) also came into my possession, and I further succeeded in tracing to the province of Siteia, in which the sites of both Praesos and Itanos are included, two interesting examples which I had observed in the collection of the Archaeological Society in the Polytechnion at Athens (see below, Figs. 32, 36). In gems of the ordinary Mycenaean class I found the whole of this Eteocretan district to be specially prolific.

In my search after these minor relics of antiquity, often, it may be remarked, of greater archaeological importance than far more imposing monuments, I was greatly aided by a piece of modern Cretan superstition. The perforated gems and seal-stones, so characteristic of Mycenaean and still earlier times, are known to the Cretan women as γαλόπετρας or 'milk-stones,' and are worn round their necks as charms of great virtue especially in time of child-bearing. It was thus possible by making a house-to-house visitation in the villages to obtain a knowledge of a large number of early engraved stones, and though I was not always able to secure the objects themselves, on account of the magic power that was supposed to attach to them, I was in nearly all cases enabled to carry off an impression of the stone. Engraved stones of other types, to be described more in detail below, with pictographic symbols, were procured by me from the neighbourhood of Knôsos and the Messarà district, and others of uncertain provenience were obtained in Candia.

The seal-stones with the linear type of symbols I found to have an equally wide distribution in the island. Two stones from the Praesos district (Figs. 29, 36), of the same angular form as those with the pictographic characters, present symbols of this 'alphabetic' class. They were the first of this type that I came across, and the discovery was the more gratifying that, on the ground of distinct resemblances in outline between simplified forms of some of the hieroglyphs observed by me in the preceding year and certain Cypriote characters, I had already ventured to predict that the pictorial forms would be found to fit on to a linear syllabary like the Asianic.[9] But

---

[9] I made this forecast in a brief announcement of the existence of the Cretan hieroglyphs communicated by me to the Hellenic Society in 1893.

here such linear characters were actually occurring, and engraved moreover on triangular and quadrangular stones identical with those presenting the pictorial types.

In the case of these quasi-alphabetic forms I was able to ascertain their application to other objects and materials. Of all the remains of ancient cities that I visited during my Cretan journey the most wonderful were those of Goulàs, as the site is at present known, lying on and between two peninsular heights, a few miles away from the sea on the Eastern side of the Province of Mirabello. Its natural haven would have been the port of St. Nicolas, in ancient times the harbour town of Latos, but the remains at Goulàs itself are, so far as I was able to observe them, so exclusively prehistoric that there seems no reason to suppose that it was ever occupied by a later Greek settlement. The remains themselves are stupendous. Wall rises within wall, terrace above terrace, and within the walls, built of the same massive blocks of local limestone in rudely horizontal tiers, the lower part of the walls of the houses and buildings are still traceable throughout. The site had been observed by Spratt,[10] but so incompletely was it known that I discovered here a second and higher akropolis with remains of primitive buildings on the summit, one containing, besides a fore-court, a chamber with *antae* recalling the ground-plan of more than one Megaron of the sixth or Mycenaean stratum of Hissarlik.[11] The whole site abounds with primaeval relics, stone vessels of early ‘Aegean type,’ bronze weapons and Mycenaean gems, of which I secured either the original or the impressions of no less than seventeen examples. In the mass of remains existing above ground, the ruins of Goulàs exceed those of any prehistoric site, either of Greece or Italy, and there cannot be a doubt that we are here in presence of one of the principal centres of the Mycenaean world.

Whilst exploring the remains of this unknown city a most remarkable piece of epigraphic evidence came across my path. A peasant who owned a little cultivated patch below the Northern akropolis, near the ruinous Byzantine Church of Hagios Andonis, pointed out a spot where he had just discovered three ancient relics which he handed over to me. One was a Mycenaean lentoid gem of cornelian, the chief design of which was a two-handled cup, the copy no doubt of a golden original, beside which in the field of the intaglio was a rayed sun and a spray of foliage. The second object was a terracotta ox (Fig. 3) of a type common in late Mycenaean deposits throughout the island, similar examples having been found in the cave of the Idaean Zeus, in that of Psychro in the heart of Mt. Lasethe and in another grotto near Sybrita in company with early bronzes. The third object was a clay cup (Fig. 4) which looked as if it had originally

---

[10] Spratt (*Travels in Crete*, ii. 129 *seqq.*) wrongly identified Goulàs with the ancient Oleros, the site of which is now known to be at Messeleri (Halbherr), also confusing it with Olous (Elunta).

[11] See Dörpfeld, *Troja*, 1893, p. 15 *seqq.* and

Pl. II. VI. A, VI. B, VI. C, and VI. G. From the recurrence of the ground-plan Dr. Dörpfeld rightly observes that the first-discovered foundations VI. A, like the others, rather represent a *Megaron* than a *Temple*.

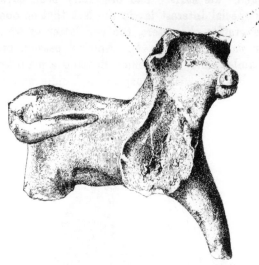

FIG. 3.—TERRACOTTA OX, GOULÀS (½ linear).

FIG. 4.—CLAY CUP WITH INCISED CHARACTERS, GOULÀS.

FIG. 4b.—CHARACTERS ON GOULÀS CUP.

been intended for a vase, but had been rudely and unevenly cut down before the clay was baked. Its surface had originally been covered by a dark varnish. But its special interest lay in the fact that on one side just below the rim are three graffito characters, the two latter of which are identical with the Cypriote *pa* and *lo* (Fig. 4*b*). Another peasant brought me from a neighbouring hamlet called Prodromos Botzano a plain terracotta vase of primitive aspect (Fig. 5), with a suspension handle and incised hatching

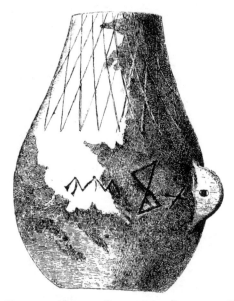

FIG. 5.—VASE WITH INCISED CHARACTERS, PRODROMOS BOTZANO.

round its neck, which showed on its body three more graffito symbols of the same kind. One of these seemed to represent the double axe-head which occurs among the hieroglyphic forms reduced to a linear outline, while the last, as in the case of the former example, was identical with the Cypriote *lo* (Fig. 5*b*). From Goulàs itself I also obtained a perforated steatite

FIG. 5*b*.—CHARACTERS ON VASE FROM PRODROMOS BOTZANO.

ornament nearly worn through with use, the face of which was also engraved with three linear marks of a more uncertain nature. It was found near the spot whence the inscribed cup and the other objects were derived.

Nor are these linear signs confined to seals and pottery. On a double-headed bronze axe (Fig. 6), procured by me in the village of Kritsà, near the

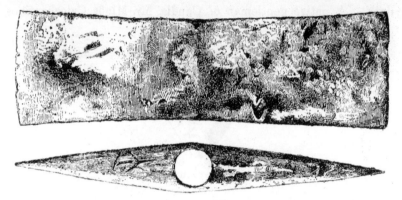

FIG. 6.—BRONZE AXE WITH INCISED CHARACTER, SELAKONOS ($\frac{1}{2}$ linear).

site of Goulàs, but said to come from Selakonos, in the Eparchy of Girapetra, I observed an engraved symbol much resembling one of the characters on the Knôsos blocks, to be described below (Fig. 9), and it is probable that other signs will eventually be found engraved on bronze implements of Mycenaean date. On a bronze axe from Delphi are engraved two symbols as sketched in Fig. 7, the first of which looks like a rude outline of a duck or some other aquatic bird.

FIG. 7.—SIGNS ON BRONZE AXE FROM DELPHI.

The history and even the ancient name of Goulàs are lost in the mist of time, and the earliest traditions of the island point rather to Knôsos, the City of Minôs, as the principal seat of power. But whatever may have been the relative parts played by the two cities in prehistoric times, it is at any rate certain that the same primitive system of writing was common to them both.

From the site of Knôsos I procured a three-sided steatite seal (Fig. 30) of the same kind as those from the Eteocretan region, presenting both pictographic and linear symbols, and also a heart-shaped jewel (Fig. 8) of amethyst with four similar characters beneath a characteristically Mycenaean engraving of a flying eagle. But at Knôsos the appearance of these linear symbols is by no means confined to seals and jewels. Already, in 1880, certain mysterious signs had been observed by Mr. W. J. Stillman [12] on the gypsum blocks that form the facing of the walls of a prehistoric building on this site, which Mr. Stillman himself was inclined to identify with the legendary Labyrinth. A native gentleman of Candia, Mr. Minôs Calochaerinos, had

FIG. 8.—ENGRAVED AMETHYST FROM KNÔSOS.

in 1878 made a partial excavation on this site and laid open some small chambers in which were a quantity of fragments of Mycenaean painted vases [13] and a number of large *pithoi* containing traces of grain, from which the place is now known to the peasants as τὰ Πιτάρια. The fragments, at present preserved in the house of their discoverer, where he kindly allowed me to examine them, are in much the same style as those found by Professor Petrie in the Palace of Akhenaten ('Khuenaten') at Tell-el-Amarna, and in the neighbouring rubbish heaps,—a parallel which gives 1400 B.C. as the approximate date for the building. Dr. Schliemann, [14] Professor Dörpfeld and Dr. Fabricius, [15] who all had occasion to examine the small portion visible above ground, were struck by the great resemblance presented by the details of the structure to those of the Palaces of Mycenae and Tiryns. Professor Halbherr recalls the *Andreion* in which the citizens of Crete used to meet together for their public meals or *syssitia*. [16]

Whether Labyrinth, Palace, or Andreion, it is evident that the prehistoric building, as yet so imperfectly known to us, belongs to the great age of Mycenae, and that its complete excavation may bring with it new revelations as to the art and culture of the Aegean peoples in the middle of the second millennium before our era. The symbols on the casing blocks of the walls, first noticed by Mr. W. J. Stillman, do not appear to have attracted the attention they seem to deserve, and have been set aside as mere ' masons' marks.' [17]   I

[12] *Second Annual Report of the Executive Committee, Arch. Inst. of America,* 1880—1881, pp. 47—49. Mr. Stillman's drawings have been reproduced in Perrot et Chipiez, *Grèce Primitive,* pp. 460, 462.

[13] Some of these were published by Haussoullier, *Bulletin de Corr. Hellénique,* 1880, pp. 124 — 127 and *Revue Archéologique* n.s. xl. (1880), p. 359 *seqq.,* cf. too Fabricius, *Athen. Mittheilungen,* 1886, p. 139 *seqq.* and Taf. III.

[14] *Verhandlungen der Berliner Anthropologischen Gesellschaft,* 1886, pp. 379—380.

[15] *Alterthümer auf Kreta, IV. Funde der Mykenäischen Epoche in Knossos (Athenische Mittheilungen,* 1886, p. 135 *seqq.*).

[16] *Researches in Crete,* in the *Antiquary,* vol. xxviii. p. 111 (Sept. 1893).

[17] Dr. Fabricius in his account of the remains (*Athen. Mitth. loc. cit.*) does not even mention them. M. Perrot indeed (*La Grèce Primitive,* p. 461), in spite of his strong ex·

paid two visits to these remains with the special object of examining these signs, the second in company with Mr. Minôs Calochaerinos and Professor Halbherr. Those that I was able to observe are reproduced (Fig. 9*a—g*) from my own drawings, supplemented in the the case of Fig. 9*h—k*, now no longer visible, by Mr. Stillman's copy. The signs occurring in pairs are placed together. The conclusion at which I arrived was that, though there need not necessarily be any objection to describing the signs as 'masons' marks,' the marks themselves, like many others of the kind, those for

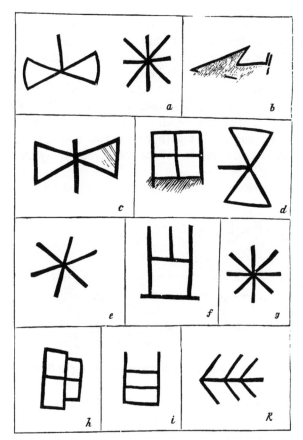

FIG. 9.—SIGNS ON BLOCKS OF MYCENAEAN BUILDING, KNÔSOS.

instance on the Phoenician walls of Eryx, are taken from a regular script and fit on in fact to the same system as the characters on the pottery and seals. In several cases indeed they occur not singly, as we should expect in ordinary masons' marks, but in groups of two. Here was the double

pression of opinion as to the non-existence of any traces of a system of writing in Mycenaean times, admits that two of the signs present a perceptible analogy to Cypriote characters. (See above, p. 274, note 7.)

axe-head reduced to a linear symbol, the rayed stars of the hieroglyphs, simplified to asterisks, and a window-like sign (Fig. 9. *d*, 1) that occurred on the Goulàs cup. One feature however was of special interest, the occurrence namely on one of the blocks of a symbol (Fig. 9. *f*), which may be described as a square with three prongs, identical with one that appears on one of the two vase-handles, referred to above as presenting graphic characters, found in Mycenae itself. Here we have an important link between the early Cretan script and that of the Peloponnese.

It is to be observed that this sign occurs on the stone, as in my sketch, upside down, and were it not from its appearance on the Mycenaean amphora, we should not have known its right position. In the same way the double-axe symbol occurs on the blocks in three different positions. The natural inference from this is that the signs were engraved on the blocks previous to their insertion in the walls of the building.

The incised marks on the slabs of the Knôsian building do not any longer stand alone. Professor Halbherr writes to me from Candia, that he has observed, 'fixed into a terrace-wall on the site of Phaestos,' a curious block on which has been engraved, together with two doubtful signs, a kind of broad arrow (Fig. 10) recalling one of the most frequent symbols both on the

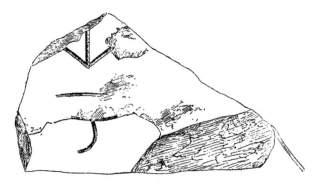

FIG. 10.—BLOCK AT PHAESTOS WITH ENGRAVED SIGNS.

hieroglyphic and linear series of the seals.[17b] He observes of this sign that not only from its regularity, but from the depth of the groove, it was in his judgment executed with a chisel. This stone lies in the neighbourhood of a spot where a very remarkable early deposit was discovered, containing engraved stones and other objects, to which it will be necessary to return when we come to consider the question of the date of the early seal-stones.[17c]

The objects obtained from this deposit are now placed together in the very interesting little Museum which has been formed by the Cretan Syllogos or Literary Society at Candia (Heraklion), mainly owing to the enterprise

---

[17b] This block is fixed into the supporting wall of a field belonging to Manolis Aposto-akis to the right of the road leading from Mires to Dibaki and opposite the Akropolis of Phaestos. Its height is 0·54m., length 0·70.

[17c] See below, p. 325.

and research of its President, Dr. Joseph Hazzidaki, whose services to Cretan archaeology deserve the widest recognition. Amongst these are two stones exhibiting engraved signs. One of these, a kind of irregular whorl (Fig. 11a and b), convex above and flat below, presents on its lower side

FIG. 11a.—ENGRAVED WHORL FROM PHAESTOS (2 diams.).

FIG. 11b.

characters so remarkably alphabetic that they might well be taken to belong to much later times—Byzantine, for instance.

But the evidence against this view must be regarded as decisive. The H and A are both found among the early marks observed by Professor Petrie on the Kahun pottery; read another way the ⊥ is a Cypriote *ve*. On the upper side of this whorl (Fig. 11a) is seen a rude engraving of a horned animal—probably a bull or ox—which is quite in the style of the animal representations of a series of very early Cretan intaglios.[18] This figure is followed by a peculiar symbol and, what is extremely remarkable, on the lower side of the stone the same symbol recurs in immediate juxtaposition to what appears to be the bull's or ox's head reduced to a linear form.[19] The engraving of the upper and lower side of the stone seems to be by the same hand. The material itself, a greenish steatite, and the irregular form both occur moreover in the case of another inscribed stone from Siphnos to be described below, bearing letters showing a very marked affinity with Cypriote. Again, every other object from the deposit in which this inscribed whorl was found seems to be of very early fabric.[19b] The *prima facie* view of the characters on this curious stone might easily lead to the conclusion that it was of much later date. But the early, irregular form and material, the rude animal, the curious association of signs unknown to the later Greek alphabet, and the place of finding point to an antiquity corresponding with that of the other relics from the same sepulchral stratum.

From the same deposit was obtained a button-like pendant of black

---

[18] I may specially cite a rudely triangular steatite, with a horned animal in a very primitive style, found with other early pendants in a grave of prae-Mycenaean date at Milato.

Compare too the animal on Fig. 18a.
[19] See below, p. 364–366.
[19b] See below, p. 104 *seqq.*

steatite engraved with linear signs (Fig. 12) and a sketch of another object of the same class has been kindly placed at my disposal by Professor Halbherr. The object in question (Fig. 13) is of a green stone somewhat more regularly formed than the other and shows on its face a K-like character,

FIG. 12 (2 diams.).

though it is uncertain which way up the sign should be set. It was found by Dr. Halbherr in a necropolis of the last Mycenaean period in Messarà consisting of oven tombs, but the pendant itself may possibly belong to a still older stratum.

FIG. 13.—ENGRAVED 'BUTTON-SEAL,' MESSARÀ (2 diams.).

My attention has been further called by Dr. Hazzidaki to a perforated terracotta object, apparently also a kind of pendant (Fig. 14), with an incised symbol consisting of a horizontal line with two cross-strokes, like the Cypriote *pa* turned on its side, from the cave of the Idaean Zeus. On a perforated disk from the site of Knôsos (Fig. 15) there occurred a sign like a Cypriote *po*. From one of a series of early cist-graves at Arvi (Arbi), on the South-East coast of the island, containing stone vessels and other relics of prae-Mycenaean date I obtained a green steatite pendant (Fig. 16) with two linear symbols, one on each side, curiously resembling an *Alef* and *Gimel*. Fig. 17, from Central Crete, a perforated triangular steatite of irregular form, also shows on two of its faces curious linear signs. Fig. 18*a* and *b* is a dark brown steatite ornament from the Messarà district, having on both sides of

C

FIG. 14.—TERRACOTTA PENDANT FROM CAVE OF IDAEAN ZEUS.

FIG. 15.—ENGRAVED DISK-BEAD, KNÔSOS (2 diams.).

FIG. 16.—STEATITE PENDANT, ARVI (2 diams.).

FIG. 17a.—PERFORATED STEATITE,   17b.
CENTRAL CRETE (2 diams.).

FIG. 18a.

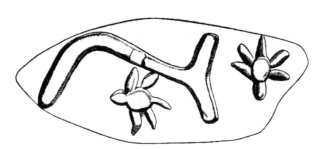

FIG. 18b.—STEATITE RELIEF, MESSARÀ (2 diams.).

FIG. 19.—SIPHNOS.

it figures in relief. On one side are what appear to be two primitive representations of animals, the style of one of which recalls the ox on the Praesos disk, while on the other face are two tortoises and an uncertain symbol grouped together like some of the pictographs on the triangular seals to be described below.

To these Cretan examples I may add a pale green perforated steatite (Fig. 19) from Siphnos, in material somewhat resembling the Phaestos disk, one side of which is engraved with characters of curiously Cypriote aspect.

§ II.—THE FACETTED STONES WITH PICTOGRAPHIC AND LINEAR SYMBOLS.

As forming a group by themselves it has been found convenient to reserve the detailed examination of the facetted stones presenting pictographic symbols for a separate section, and at the same time to place with them the prism-shaped seals of the same type with more linear characters.

Another form of bead-seal and two examples of lentoid gems with pictographic groups are also added.

The facetted stones themselves are of three principal types, all of them perforated along their major axis.

I.—Three-sided or prism-shaped (Fig. 20 *a* and *b*). This type is divided into two varieties—one elongated (*a*) the other more globular (β).

FIG. 20*a*.—(2 diams.).　　　　　FIG. 20*b*.—(2 diams.).

II.—Four-sided equilateral.

III.—Four-sided with two larger faces.

IV.—With one engraved side, the upper part being ornamented with a convoluted relief (Fig 21).

FIG. 21.—(2 diams.).

This form may perhaps be regarded as a later development of an earlier type of Cretan bead, the upper part of which is carved into the shape of two Nerita shells lying end to end with a common whorl, a specimen of which was found in the Phaestos deposit above referred to.

The other stones, which are of ordinary Mycenaean forms including the lentoid type, are grouped with the above as Class V. The figures are taken from casts, so that, assuming that the originals were seals, this gives the right direction of the symbols. In some cases however it is not easy to decide which way up the impression should be shown, and the order in which the sides are arranged is for the most part arbitrary. When one side presents a single type of an evidently ideographic character it has been given the first place, and at times a boustrophêdon arrangement seems to be traceable. In Fig. 23 for instance, the first side seems to run from right to left, the second from left to right, and the third again from right to left. The drawings were executed by Mr. F. Anderson with the guidance of magnified photographs from casts, and the stones are in all cases enlarged to two diameters. Effects due to the technique of the early gem-engraver's art, such as the constant tendency to develop globular excrescences, must be mentally deducted from the pictographs. Unless otherwise indicated, the stones or their impressions were obtained in Crete by the writer.

Class I.

THREE-SIDED OR PRISM-SHAPED.

21c.   21b.   21a.

FIG. 21.

A. (Fig. 21).—Brown steatite.   Crete.   Uncertain locality.

22a.

22b.

22c.

FIG. 22.

B. (Fig. 22).—Green jasper.   Province of Siteia. Crete,

23a.

23b.

23c

FIG. 23.

C. (Fig. 23).—White cornelian. Eastern Crete.

24a.   24b.   24c.

FIG. 24.

D. (Fig. 24).—White cornelian. Eastern Crete.

25c.   25b.   25a.

FIG. 25.

E. (Fig. 25).—Crete. (Berlin Museum.)

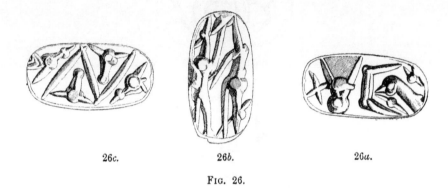

26c.   26b.   26a.

FIG. 26.

F. (Fig. 26).—Red cornelian.   Crete.   Province of Siteia.

27c.   27b.   27a.

FIG. 27.

G. (Fig. 27).—Brown steatite.   Crete.   Uncertain locality.

Sides *b* and *c* contain what appear to be purely decorative designs.

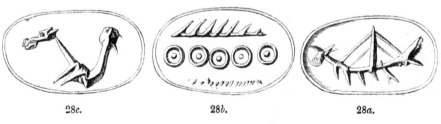

28c.   28b.   28a.

FIG. 28.

H. (Fig. 28).—Steatite.   Crete.   Uncertain locality.

29a.

29b.

29c.

FIG. 29.

I. (Fig. 29).—White steatite.   Praesos.

FIG. 30a.

FIG. 30b.

FIG. 30c.

FIG. 30.

J. (Fig. 30).—Grey steatite.   Knosos.   (From a sketch.)

31c.   31b.   31a.

FIG. 31.

K. (Fig. 31).—This stone belongs to the more globular type, Class I. *b.*
Crete. (Berlin Museum.)

Class II.

FOUR-SIDED EQUILATERAL STONES.

32d.   32c.   32b   32a.

FIG. 32.

A. (Fig. 32).—Red cornelian. Crete (Ashmolean Museum; Mr.
Greville Chester; wrongly labelled as 'from Sparta,' see p. 136).

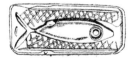

33a.

33b.

33c.

33d.

FIG. 33.

B. (Fig. 33).—Crete.   Province of Siteia.   (Polytechnion, Athens.)

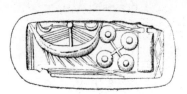

34a.

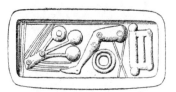

34b.

34c.

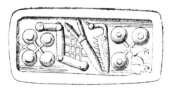

34d.

FIG. 34.

C. (Fig. 34).—Crete. (Berlin Museum.)

35*a.*

35*b.*

35*c.*

35*d.*

FIG. 35.

D. (Fig 35).—Green jasper.   Crete.   Palaekastro, near site of Itanos.

36*a.*

36*b.*

36*c.*

36*d.*

FIG. 36.

E. (Fig. 36).—Steatite.   Province of Siteia.   (Polytechnion, Athens.)
Sides *a* and *c* contain decorative designs.

Class III.

FOUR-SIDED STONES WITH TWO LARGER FACES.

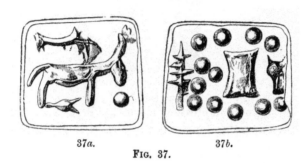

37*a.*   37*b.*

FIG. 37.

A. (Fig. 37).—Green steatite. Central Crete. This stone properly belongs to an earlier class.

Class IV.

STONES WITH A SINGLE FACE: THE UPPER PART CONVOLUTED.

FIG 38.

A. (Fig. 38).—White cornelian. Eastern Crete.

Class V.

STONES OF ORDINARY MYCENAEAN TYPE.

FIG. 39.

A. (Fig. 39).—From impression taken by Professor Sayce at Athens. This form of gem was in use for the besils of rings in Mycenaean times.

FIG. 40.

B. (Fig. 40).—Brown steatite. Knôsos. This and the following are ordinary types of perforated lentoid bead but of very early fabric.

FIG. 41.

C. (Fig. 41).—Black steatite. Messarà district.

§ III.—EVIDENCES OF A PICTOGRAPHIC SCRIPT.

IT is impossible to believe that the signs on these stones were simply idle figures carved at random. Had there not been an object in grouping several signs together it would have been far simpler for the designer to have chosen single figures or continuous ornament to fill the space at his disposal. As it is, single figures or continuous ornament are occasionally introduced on the vacant sides of stones where it was not necessary to cover the whole stone with symbolic characters; and in the same way small ornamental forms are found in some cases filling, for decorative purposes, the spaces between the symbols. In Fig. 22 one side is purely decorative; in Figs. 27 and 36, two sides, and such features as the small chevrons in the vacant spaces of Fig. 31c, or the network behind the designs on Figs. 33a and 34c and d, are obviously supplementary ornaments. But these extraneous features only bring out more clearly the fact that the signs themselves are introduced with a definite meaning, and are in fact a form of script. A method and intention in the choice and arrangement of the symbols is moreover perceptible, quite incompatible with the view that they are mere meaningless ornaments.

The signs themselves are chosen from a conventional field. Limited as is the number of stones that we have to draw from, it will be found that certain symbols are continually recurring as certain letters or syllables or words would recur in any form of writing. Thus the human eye appears four times and on as many different stones, the 'broad arrow' seven times, and another uncertain instrument (No. 16 of the list given in the succeeding section) as much as eleven times. The choice of symbols is evidently restricted by some practical consideration, and while some objects are of frequent occurrence, others equally obvious are conspicuous by their absence. But an engraver filling the space on the seals for merely decorative purposes would not thus have been trammelled in his selection.

Two other characteristics of hieroglyptic script are also to be noted. The first is the frequent use of abbreviated symbols, such as the head for the whole animal, the flower or spray for the plant. The second is the appearance of gesture-language in graphic form—an invaluable resource of early pictography for the expression of ideas and emotions. Amongst such may be noted the human figure with arms held down (Fig. 36b), the crossed arms with open palms and thumbs turned back (Fig. 31b), and, closely allied to this, the bent single arm with open palm (Fig. 35d). Such features, again, as the wolf's head with protruding tongue—also found on Hittite monuments—or the dove pluming its wing, have probably a significance beyond the mere indication of the animal or bird.

The symbols occur almost exclusively in groups of from two to seven; the most frequent however are of two or of three, which seems to show that the characters thus appearing had a syllabic value. Certain fixed principles, also, are traceable in the arrangements of the symbols in the several groups. Some signs are almost exclusively found at the beginning or the end of a line. The human eye appears thus three times out of four; the instrument No. 16 of the list below occupies the extremity of the group in seven, or perhaps eight, cases where it occurs. The same two symbols more-over are seen on different stones in the same collocation. Thus the horns and four-rayed star occur in close proximity on the stones (Fig. 23*b* and 32*b*) from Crete. The instrument (No. 16) above referred to occurs five times on as many different stones in collocation with the ' broad arrow.' The arrow-head, again, is twice placed beside the ψ-like sign No. 54 (Figs. 23*b* and 35*a*). In four cases where the bent leg makes its appearance (Figs. 22*b*, 25*a*, 34*b* and Supplement, p. 136), it is in immediate contiguity with a symbol that seems to stand for a door or gate. Such collocations in the small number of instances at our disposal are alone sufficient to exclude the supposition that the signs on these stones were engraved haphazard for decorative purposes.

It further appears, when we come to file the several columns, as on the Babylonian principle they would follow one another in the impression of a seal, that in several cases a boustrophêdon arrangement has been adopted which recalls that of early Greek writing. This is specially noticeable in Figs. 22, 23, 33, as well as in Fig. 34, where by the analogy of other Myce-naean gems from Crete representing ships the vessel must be taken as going in the direction in which the oars slope. It seems usual to begin from right to left.

That these seals were designed to convey information regarding their owners in a primitive form of writing is clearly brought out by another phenomenon with which we have to deal. On Fig. 36*d* the place of the pictographic symbols is taken by linear characters which no one will deny represent actual letters, and which fit on in fact to an Aegean or Mycenaean syllabary the existence of which can be demonstrated from inde-pendent sources. This phenomenon must certainly be taken to throw a retrospective light on the hieroglyphic forms that replace the letters on the bulk of these stones. It will be further shown in the course of this inquiry that a certain proportion of these pictographic signs reduced to linear forms actually live on in this Aegean syllabary.

In a succeeding section [19a] attention will be called to a still earlier class of Cretan seal-stones presenting for the most part the same typical tri-angular form as those of Class I. already described. These more primitive stones, which cannot in fact be separated by any definite line of demarcation from the later series, throw a valuable light on the original elements out of which the more formalized pictographic system finally grew. In some cases the same symbols are actually seen in a more primitive stage of development. But on this earlier class the more purely pictorial and ideographic elements

---

[19a] See p. 324 *seqq.* The stones, Figs. 21, 37, 39, 40, might perhaps with greater propriety have been grouped with this earlier series.

D

are naturally preponderant and the personal relation in which the seals stand to their owners is clearly revealed. They seem indeed to be descriptive of his individual character as an owner of flocks and herds, a merchant, a huntsman or a warrior.

These more naive delineations, of a ruder stage of culture, supply a welcome clue to the interpretation of such ideographic elements as survive in the more conventional forms with which we are at present dealing. Here too we may often see a reference to the avocation or profession of the owner of the seal and may venture to conclude that the more purely symbolic characters have a personal application. Thus for example Fig. 34, exhibiting at the beginning of one column a ship with two crescent moons above it, may be reasonably supposed to have been the signet of one who undertook long voyages. Fig. 24, with the pig and door, would have belonged to some one who owned herds of swine: in which case the two figures of the axe and kid on the other face may contain the elements of the owner's own name. The fish at the head of Fig. 33 may indicate a fisherman. The seal-stone represented in Fig. 23, with the adze and other implements—including one in which I have ventured to recognize the template of a decorative artist,—probably belonged to a member of a masons' guild. The harp on Fig. 31 suggests a musician. It is possible that the individual element of ownership, which on the earlier class is brought out by the complete human figure, may be elsewhere indicated by the human eye alone, which is of frequent occurrence in these stones.

§ IV.—Classification and Comparison of the Symbols.

In the following list I have included all the above signs that have any claim to be regarded as of hieroglyphic value, excluding the small obviously ornamental devices that are occasionally found filling in the space between the symbols, but including one or two like the S-shaped figures that may after all belong to the same decorative or supplemental category. It will be seen from the arrangement adopted that the symbols, where it is possible to recognize their meaning, fall into regular classes like the Hittite or the Egyptian.

The Human Body and its Parts.

1   Fig. 36b. Ideograph of a man standing alone, with his arms held downwards, perhaps denoting ownership. It is followed by linear characters on another facet of the stone. Human figures in this position are frequent on Cypriote cylinders. A similar figure also occurs on a cone from Ramleh, near Jaffa, in the Ashmolean Collection.

2　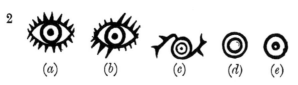

(a)　　　(b)　　　(c)　　　(d)　　　(e)

Figs. 29a, 32d, 34b and c, 35b and c, and 38. The eye appears twice in conjunction with No. 16. As an indication of meaning we may compare Egyptian ⌣ *ân ;* also determinative of 'sight,' 'watching,' &c. On the Hittite monuments the eye does not seem to be separately portrayed. On the inscriptions of Hamath and Jerabis (Wright, *Emp. of the Hittites,* Pl. I. H. 1, line 1, and Pl. VIII. A., line 1) the upper part of a figure of a man is represented, with his finger apparently pointing to his eye.

In the delineation of this symbol on the Cretan seal-stones, four distinct stages are perceptible : (1) the whole eye with the lashes all round ; (2) the whole eye with the lashes fully drawn on two diagonal sides of the eye only, elsewhere only faintly indicated ; (3) what appears to be an abbreviated form of the latter type ; (4) the pupil and iris only, indicated by concentric circles. In one case (Fig. 35) this latter type occurs on the same stone as the complete eye in a place where it would have been impossible to insert the full symbol.

It is, however, difficult to distinguish this latter simplified form, consisting of concentric circles with or without a central dot, from what appears to be a solar symbol. (See below, No. 62.)

3　Fig. 31b. Another ideograph taken from gesture-language. The sign may have indicated 'ten' or any multiple of ten : thus any great number. So far as the crossing of the arms goes, the symbol may be compared with the two confronted figures that occur twice on a Jerabis monument (Wright, *op. cit.* Pl. IX.).

4　Fig. 35d. Also a gesture-sign. The Egyptian open hand indicates a palm measure. The forepart of the arm with open hand is seen on one of the Jerabis inscriptions (Wright, *op. cit.* Pl. VIII. B. 1. 2). Compare, too, the hand and forearm sculptured on a rock at Itanos above an archaic Greek inscription (Comparetti, *Leggi di Gortyna,* &c., p. 442, No. 206).

5　Figs. 22b, 25a, 34b. The bent leg ⌇ in Egyptian = *pat, ret, men,* &c., as a determinative, is applied to actions of the leg, as 'marching' and 'approaching,' and to agrarian measurements, as *arura,* 'an acre.' Among Hittite symbols only the lower part of the leg is found, apparently booted. Cp. *Kolitolu Yaila.* So far as style is concerned, the greatest resemblance is presented by a bent human leg seen in the field of a gem from the lower city of Mycenae (Tomb 10, 'Εφ. 'Αρχ. 1888, Pl. X. 9).

6 Fig. 32*d*. Possibly = a rump.

ARMS, IMPLEMENTS, AND INSTRUMENTS.

7 Fig. 32*b* and cf. 41. Resembles an arm holding a curved instrument. As such it may be compared with the Egyptian determinative 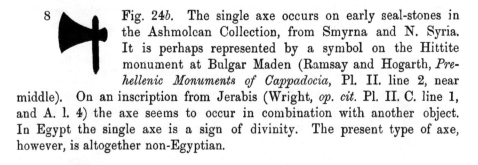 = a hand holding a club (*neχt*), applied to forcible action. The forepart of the arm holding weapons or implements is common among Hittite symbols.

8 Fig. 24*b*. The single axe occurs on early seal-stones in the Ashmolean Collection, from Smyrna and N. Syria. It is perhaps represented by a symbol on the Hittite monument at Bulgar Maden (Ramsay and Hogarth, *Pre-hellenic Monuments of Cappadocia*, Pl. II. line 2, near middle). On an inscription from Jerabis (Wright, *op. cit.* Pl. II. C. line 1, and A. l. 4) the axe seems to occur in combination with another object. In Egypt the single axe is a sign of divinity. The present type of axe, however, is altogether non-Egyptian.

9 Fig. 37*b*. Perhaps an early form of double axe-head.

10 Figs. 23*b*, 39. The double axe is a form altogether foreign to Egypt. As a Hittite hieroglyph it has been recently detected on an inscription, and it is seen repeated in pairs on a Cypriote cylinder (Cesnola, *Salaminia*, Fig. 118, p. 128). It occurs as a symbol in the field of a Mycenaean gold ring (Schliemann, *Mycenae*, Fig. 530, p. 354), where it has been connected with the cult of Zeus Labrandeus. It also forms the principal type of some Mycenaean gems found in Crete—one from near Girapetra, the other from Goulàs. Bronze axes of the above form are common in the votive deposits of the Cretan caves like that of the Idaean Zeus and of Psychro on Mount Lasethe (see above, Fig. 6).

11 Fig. 33*d*. The dagger symbol appears in two forms among Egyptian hieroglyphs, ⚓ *bakasu* and ⚓ *χaa*. When it occurs among Hittite signs it ∇ is grasped ∪ by a hand (Hamath Wright, *op. cit.* Pl, III. H. iv. line 1, and Jerabis, *op. cit.* Pl. XII. Fig. 1, l. 2). The roundness of the pommel of the hilt on the Cretan sign is probably simply due to the early gem-engraver's technique, which relies greatly on the drill.

12 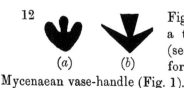 Fig. 21*b*. Arrow-head. The form *b* occurs on a triangular stone of a somewhat earlier class (see below, p. 344, Fig. 68), but is here inserted for comparison. Compare, too, the sign on the

(*a*)   (*b*)

Mycenaean vase-handle (Fig. 1).

13 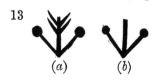 Figs. 34*c*, 23*b*, 24*c*, 30*b*, 32*a*, 33*b*, 35*a*. The 'arrow' with a short shaft is frequent on these stones, one variety (13*a*) showing the feather-shaft. Similar figures are occasionally seen in the field of Mycenaean gems found in the

(*a*)   (*b*)

island, where they represent arrows of the chase about to strike wild goats or other animals. The Hittite hieroglyphic series presents some close parallels.

Jerabis (*op. cit.* Pl. VIII. D. 1. 4,   Gurun and Bulgar Maden (R. and H.
and Pl. X. 1. 4).   Pl. II. and Pl. IV. Fig. 2).

14 Figs. 23*b*, 35*c*. This symbol must be taken in connexion with the next, in which a palmette with curving base is inserted into its arch. Reasons will be given below (p. 319) for identifying this with the 'template' used in constructing a design formed of palmettes and returning spirals, which on other evidence seems to have been employed in Crete in Mycenaean days. It may therefore be a badge of a decorative artist.

15 Fig. 23*a*.

16 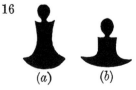 Figs. 21*b*, 22*a*, 23*a*, 23*c*, 25*c*, 32*a*, 33*b*, 34*c*, 35*a*, 35*b*, 38. This symbol, which is the most frequent of all, occurring no less than eleven times in the present series, may represent an instrument—like an arbelon—for cutting leather. Or it may possibly be compared with a tool such

(*a*)   (*b*)

as the Egyptians used for hollowing out vessels, and which seems to be represented by the Egyptian character *Ub* ☐ (See De Rougé, *Chrestomathie Égyptienne*, p. 75.) Compare also *Shen* ⚭ = a chisel. ⚲ The projecting shoulders recall a form of bronze celt. ☐

17   Figs. 34*a* and 23*b*. Apparently another instrument of the same class as the above.

18   Fig. 32*d*. This form may be compared with the Egyptian ⌂ = a mallet, determinative of 'to fabricate' or 'build.' The Hittite ⊏⊐ from Gurun (R. and H. Pl. IV. 2, line 2) affords a close parallel to this and the above.

19   Figs. 31*b*, 31*c*. This highly interesting symbol represents a primitive form of musical instrument which, though it at first sight rather recalls a lyre from its horn-shaped sides, is essentially a harp, its opposite sides being connected by three strings and not by a solid cross-piece. Regarded as a harp, however, it presents an entirely new type, apparently standing in the same relation to the Asiatic horn-bow as the simple forms of African and other harps do to the wooden bow. It was, however, played with a *plectrum* which, as in the case of primitive lyres among savages at the present day, is here seen attached to the framework of the instrument. Although this symbol must be classified as a harp, and not as a lyre, we may well ask ourselves whether an instrument of this form, derived from the two-horned Asiatic bow, may not have influenced—contaminated, as mythologists would say—the form of the Greek lyre, the horn-shaped sides of which are not essential to that form of instrument.

20 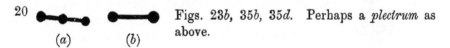   Figs. 23*b*, 35*b*, 35*d*. Perhaps a *plectrum* as above.

(*a*)   (*b*)

21   Fig. 25*a*. A club or sceptre. Compare the Egyptian ⊏⊐O = club, ⊏⊐Oᵖ = mace, symbol of 'brilliancy' and 'whiteness.'

22   Fig. 23*c*. There can be little doubt that this symbol represents an adze or some similar tool with a wooden handle. The handle shows affinities with the Egyptian a kind of adze or plane, which = *stp*, 'to judge' or 'approve.' It may also be compared with the Hittite (Jerabis, Wright, *op. cit.* Pl. IX. lines 7, 8). Long adzes are among the most typical forms of bronze implements found in Crete. They are found in Mycenaean deposits, and one in my possession from the Cave of Psychro is 11·35 inches in length. It is probable that the end of the wooden handle of the Cretan implement represented above was shaped like the hind leg and hoof of an animal, as in the case of many Egyptian tools.

23  Fig. 34*d*. Saw, shaped like the jaw of an animal, probably formed of wood set with flint flakes. Compare the Egyptian

 = saw. For a somewhat similar saw of wood set with flint teeth from Kahun, see Petrie, *Illahun, Kahun, and Gurob,* Pl. VII. Fig. 27.

HOUSES AND HOUSEHOLD UTENSILS.

24 Figs. 22*b*, 24*a*, 25*a*, 29*b*. Gate, door, or part of a fence. No. 2 in connexion with a pig.

(*a*)   (*b*)

25 Figs. 30*a*, 32*c*, 36*d*. Perhaps variant of above, but cf. the Egyptian symbol for 'shutter'

26 Fig. 34*b*. Gate or shutter.

27 Fig. 32*c*. Fence.

28 Fig. 39. This vase evidently represents a metal original closely resembling the Oriental *ibrik,* which serves an ewer for pouring and sprinkling water. Vessels of this shape form the principal type of a class of Mycenaean gems specially common in Eastern Crete (see below, p. 370), sometimes fitted with a conical cover like Persian ewers of the same kind. The curving spout recalls that of an Egyptian libation-vase— *Kabh* = 'libation,' 'sweet water'—but a simpler parallel is found in the ordinary water-vessel *num* = 'water.' It is probable that the Cretan sign also stands for 'water'; indeed, on the lentoid gems referred to, this vase and others closely akin, with high beaked spouts, are seen beside a plant or spray.[19b] All this clearly indicates the purpose of watering.

29 Figs. 32*c*, 31*c*. This form of vessel is of ceramic character, and the seal on which it occurs belongs to an early class. It corresponds with a primitive type of high-beaked vases of very wide distribution, extending from Cyprus and the

---

[19b] In the case of a closely allied form of vase with two handles the spray is seen inserted in the mouth of the vessel. On a gem from Goulàs a vase of this kind is seen beside a plant, above which is a rayed disc indicating the midday sun.

Troad to the Aegean Islands and the mainland of Greece. They occur at
Hissarlik, and in the early cist-graves of Amorgos of prae-Mycenaean date, and
I found part of the beaked spout of one of equally early fabric on the site
of Praesos. Vases of this form are seen on the most primitive class of
Cretan engraved gems, going back to the third millennium B.C. (see
p. 332), and continue — taking at times a more metallic form — into
the Mycenaean period. On two Vaphio gems ('Εφ. 'Αρχ. 1890, Pl. X. 35
36) a closely allied *prochous* is seen in the hands of the mysterious beast-
headed daemons of Mycenaean art, who in one case are engaged in watering
nurseling palm-trees. Another representation of the same form of vase
occurs above two bulls in the field of a gem from Tomb 27 of the lower
town of Mycenae ('Εφ. 'Αρχ. 1888, Pl. X. 24).

30   Fig. 40.   This symbol belongs to the same class as the above.

31   Fig. 40.   Possibly some kind of vessel.

MARINE SUBJECTS.

32      Figs. 34*a*, 28*a*.   The first of these vessels
is accompanied with two crescents, one on
either side of the mast—perhaps a sign of
time as applied to the duration of a voyage
(*a*)   (*b*)   (see below, No. 65).   One ship has seven
oars visible, the other six. In form these vessels show a great resemblance
to those which appear as the principal type on a class of Mycenaean lentoid
gems, specimens of which are found in Crete. One of these in my possession
shows fifteen oars and a double rudder, and perhaps an upper row of oars.
The double end of the first example—like an open beak—may recall the
swan-headed ships of the confederate invaders of Egypt 'from the middle of
the sea' in Rameses III.'s time as seen on the frescoes of Medinet Habou. In
the present case, however, no yards are visible.

33   Fig. 33*a*.   Apparently a tunny-fish: the hatched-work
behind may indicate a net. Fish as hieroglyphic symbols
are common to Egypt and Chaldaea. It looks as if tunny-fisheries had
existed off the Cretan coast in Mycenaean times. The well-known gem with a
fisherman in the British Museum (*Gem Catalogue*, 80, Pl. A) may refer to the
same industry; and tunny-fish occur on two more Cretan gems of Mycenaean
date in the same collection. A fish of the same type occurs as a symbol
on Cypriote cylinders (cf. *Salaminia*, Pl. XIV. 48).

34 Fig. 39. Also apparently a fish. The head is more rounded than No. 33, but this may be due to rudeness of design. Fish of the same rude form are seen on Cypriote cylinders (cf. Cesnola, *Salaminia*, Pl. XIV. 48).

ANIMALS AND BIRDS.

35 Fig. 33c. Head of he-goat. This symbol presents a remarkable similarity to the Hittite hieroglyph of the same object $\searrow$, the value of which from its occurrence on the bi- $\frown$ lingual seal of Tarkutimme (Tarkondêmos) in Hittite and cuneiform characters is known to represent the syllables *Tarrik* or *Tarku* (Sayce, *Trans. Soc. Bibl. Arch.* Vol. VII. Pt. II. (1881), p. 297, and *Emp. of Hittites*, p. 182; Theo. Pinches, *ib.* p. 220, and *Trans. Soc. Bibl. Arch.* March 3, 1885; and cf. Halévy, *Rev. Sém.* 1893, p. 55 *seqq.*). The element 'Tarrik,' again, in the name of this prince, seems to refer to the god *Tark* (cf. Ramsay and Hogarth, *Prehellenic Monuments of Cappadocia*, p. 9 *seqq.*). The Egyptian goat's-head sign is of a different character. The neck is given as well as the head, and there is no beard.

36 Fig. 37a. Bull or Ox. The seal on which it occurs is of primitive type.

37 Fig. 24b. A doe or kid.

38 Figs. 23b, 32b. Apparently intended for deer-horns.

39 Fig. 26a. Horned head of an uncertain animal, apparently an ox.

40 Fig. 21a. This appears to be rather a *bucranium* or skull of a bull or ox, than the actual head of the animal. As an ornament of the reliefs of altars the *bucranium* occurs already in Mycenaean art. This appears from a lentoid gem in the British

Museum, on which is seen an animal of the goat kind freshly slaughtered, with a dagger thrust into its shoulder, lying on an altar or sacrificial bench, the front of which is adorned with four *bucrania* much resembling the above. In this case, to complete the parallel with later classical reliefs, fillets attached to the extremities of the horns are seen hanging down between the skulls.

41 Fig. 34*d*. This symbol must be regarded as uncertain. It is placed here, however, as showing a great resemblance to the Hittite sign which has been interpreted as an elongated form of the ⋁ ass's head. (Palanga.)

42 Fig. 37*b*. Perhaps a variant of the above.

43 Fig. 24*a*. Pig. A similar ideograph occurs on a three-sided stone of the earlier Cretan type presented to the Ashmolean Museum by Mr. J. L. Myres.

44 Figs. 23*a*, 32*b*. Wolf's head with the tongue hanging out. This symbol shows a remarkable likeness to the Hittite ⟶ (Jerabis, *op. cit.* Pl. VIII. D. l. 3, Pl. IX. ⟶ l. 3), where again we find the same protruding tongue.

45 Fig. 31*a*. Dove pluming its wing.

46 Fig. 40. Perhaps variant form of above.

47 Fig. 39. Bird standing. Birds in a somewhat similar position occur among the Hittite symbols at Jerabis and Bulgar Maden, and are frequent in Egyptian hieroglyphics.

48 Fig. 26*a*. Apparently a bird's head. Heads of various kinds of birds are common among Egyptian hieroglyphics.

49 Fig. 32c. This symbol apparently consists of two birds heads turned in opposite directions.

50

(a)   (b)

Figs. 28c, 30a. Perhaps a conventionalized sea-horse. The uppermost symbol on Fig. 18b (No. 76 below) may be a simplification of this. Compare ⌒ on a 'Hittite' seal-stone from Smyrna. A very similar form occurs on an early truncated cone from Tartûs.

51 On the steatite relief (Fig. 18b). Apparently a tortoise.

VEGETABLE FORMS.

52 Fig. 34b.

53 Fig. 25b.

54 Figs. 23b, 33d, 35a, 35c. This may perhaps be regarded as an abbreviated form of one of the above, with possibly a differentiated meaning. The form is common to the Hittite monuments, occurring at Jerabis, (Wright, op. cit. Pl. VIII. B l. 5) in a more floral, and also (op. cit. Pl. XIX. 6) in a geometrical form; while at Bulgar Maden (Ramsay and Hogarth, Prehellenic Monuments of Cappadocia, Pl. II. l. 3, beginning) it forms a purely linear sign . The same, or a closely allied symbol, is also seen on the lion of Marash (Wright, op. cit. Pl. XXVII. 111, l. 1).

55 Fig. 25b.

56 Fig. 31c. Perhaps a lily. This form is more pictorial than the others. Compare the Hittite 🜲 Hamath (Wright, *op. cit.* Pl. IV. ll. 2 and 3).

57 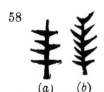 Fig. 32d. I have placed this symbol, as completed, amongst floral forms from its apparent analogy to the Hittite as seen on the monument at Ivriz (Ramsay and Hogarth, *Prehellenic Monuments of Cappadocia,* Pl. III.). The dot which occurs above both symbols may be reasonably interpreted as representing the head of a stamen or pistil, as those of the lily, No. 56.

58 Figs. 37b, 40. Tree symbol. On a Mycenaean lentoid gem, now in the Museum of the Syllogos at Candia, a votary is seen blowing a conch-shell before an altar, behind which is a sacred grove with trees in the same conventional style. A similar degeneration of the sacred tree occurs on Cypriote cylinders.

(a)   (b)

59 Fig. 28b, repeated. Spray or branch, and the same is seen duplicated on Fig. 29c.

HEAVENLY BODIES AND DERIVATIVES.

60 Fig. 33c. Day-star, or sun, with eight revolving rays.

61 Fig. 27a (the rays more revolving). Day-star, or sun, with twelve rays. Star-like symbols occur on Syrian and Asianic seal-stones.

62 Fig. 35b. This symbol, with the tangential offshoots suggesting revolution, seems to fit on to No. 60 and to be of solar import. For the concentric circles as a solar emblem compare the Egyptian ⊙ *Sep* = times (*vices*), and the circle with a central dot is also the Chinese symbol for sun. The eye symbol, No. 4, approaches this very closely.

63   Fig. 35*d*. This form suggests a combination of solar and lunar symbols.

64   Fig. 32*b* and cf. 39. Star of four rays. This symbol is frequent on Cypriote cylinders.

65   Two small crescent-moons are seen on either side of the mast of the vessel on Fig. 34*a*. They perhaps indicate duration of time—months—as applied to the length of a voyage.

GEOGRAPHICAL OR TOPOGRAPHICAL.

66
(*a*)   (*b*)

Figs. 35*d*, 25*b*. Apparently variants of the same symbol which seems to represent a widely distributed pictograph for mountains and valleys, and so country or land. On the boss of Tarriktimme (Tarkondêmos) = country (Sayce, *Trans. Bibl. Arch.* Vol. VII. Pt. II. (1887), p. 297 △△△ *seqq*; and cf. Halévy, *Rev. Sémitique*, 1893, p. 55 *seqq*.). It is found again in Jerabis (Wright, *op. cit.* Pl. IX. J. II. 1. 1) and apparently on the monument near Bulgar Maden (R. and H. *Prehellenic Monuments*, &c., Pl. II. 1. 2) △△.

The Egyptian ⌐⌐ *men* = mountain is applied in the same way as a determinative ⌐⌐ for 'districts' and 'countries.' As *snut* = granary, it reappears, with one or two heaps of corn in ⌐⌐ the middle, in the simple sense of a 'plot of ground.' The Accadian symbol, again, signifying a plot of ground, exhibits a form closely parallel to the above.   ⊠

And in this connexion a truly remarkable coincidence is observable between the pictographic symbolism of old Chaldaea and that of the Cretans of the Mycenaean period. The linear form of the Accadian *Ut-tu* ⊠ shows a sun above the symbol of the ground with a plant growing out of it. But on specimens of Mycenaean gems observed by me in Eastern Crete, side by side with the vase for watering already referred to, are seen symbolic or conventional representations of the plant growing out of the ground, recalling the Accadian version almost *totidem lineis* ⋎⋎ on amygdaloid cornelian; Zero (near Praesos). ⋎ on amygdaloid ⋎⋎ cornelian; Goulàs. In another case the ewer ⌐⌐ divides the two symbols ⋎ ⋎ on an almond-shaped stone of the same character; Girapetra.

Geometrical Figures.

67   Figs. 23*b*, 23*c*, 25*a*, 25*c*, 33*d*, 34*b*, 38. This sign may be simply a supplementary figure. On Fig. 38 it is thrice repeated with the sign No. 16, and might, like the similar Egyptian sign ✕, indicate multiplication.

68   Figs. 34*a*, 34*d*. This may be an intercalated sign, perhaps of the nature of a break between words.

69   Figs. 21*a*, 23*c*. Repeated in two directions on Fig. 23*c*. This, too, is possibly an ornamental insertion, but it may however be compared with the Egyptian ⟨sign⟩, a coil of thread, signifying 'to reel.'

(*a*) (*b*)

70   Fig. 24*c*. This may be the same as No. 69 with an additional ornamental flourish.

Uncertain Symbols.

71   Figs. 31*b*, 35*c*. The late Hittite sign ⟨sign⟩ occurs at Gurun (R. and H. *op. cit.* Pl. IV. 2, 1. 2), and perhaps in the inscription near Bulgar Maden (*op. cit.* Pl. II. 1. 3).

(*a*)   (*b*)

72   Fig. 27*a*.

73   Fig. 25*c*.

74   Fig. 25*c*. Somewhat fractured below.

75   *Fig. 34d.* A certain analogy is presented by the Hittite sign  Hamath (Wright, *op. cit.* Pl. I. H. II. l. 2), Jerabis (*op. cit.* Pl. VIII. B. l. 5), and on the 'Niobe' (Ed. Gollob. in *op. cit.* Pl. XXII.).

76   *Fig. 18b.* On the steatite relief (Fig. 18*b*); possibly a conventionalized form of No. 50.

77   *Fig. 26a.*

78   *Fig. 25a.* Perhaps a variant of No. 69.

79   *Fig. 33c.* This symbol presents a certain resemblance to the Hittite forms Hamath (Wright, *op. cit.* Pl. I. l. 1, Pl. II. H. III. l. 1, Pl. IV. H. V. l. 1); Jerabis (*op. cit.* Pl. VIII. J. I. A. l. 3, B. l. 2); Bulgar Maden (R. and H. *op. cit.* Pl. II. l. 3); Gurun (*op. cit.* Pl. IV. 1).

80   *Fig. 22a.* This recalls the Egyptian ✕ = 'skein of thread,' the determinative for 'linen,' 'bind- ○ ing,' &c.. Compare, too, the twisted cord *sen* = 'to turn back,' and *kes*, the tied up bundle ✕ = 'to bury.' On the Hittite silver seal procured at Bor, near Tyana (Ramsay and Hogarth, *Prehellenic Monuments of Cappadocia*, p. 17, Fig. 2), occurs the sign 𓎛 identical with the Cretan.

81   *Figs. 35c, 35d.*

(a)   (b)

82   *Fig. 32c.* This symbol, if rightly completed, recalls the Egyptian ✕◇✕ = *Net*, which serves especially to write the name of Neith the Goddess of Sais; also 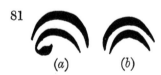 = *āt*, and its abbreviated form, sometimes described as a 'twisted cord,'

It will be seen from the above list that there are some eighty-two symbols classified under the following heads:

The human body and its parts	6
Arms, implements and instruments	17
Parts of houses and household utensils	8
Marine subjects	3
Animals and birds	17
Vegetable forms	8
Heavenly bodies and derivatives	6
Geographical or topographical signs	1
Geometrical figures	4
Uncertain symbols	12

The numerous comparisons made with Egyptian hieroglyphs in the course of the above analysis do not by any means involve the conclusion that we have in the Cretan signs merely their blundered imitation. Where such occur, as in the case of a well-known class of Phoenician and of some Cypriote Greek objects, we are confronted with very different results. Had there been any attempt to copy Egyptian cartouches or inscriptions, we should infallibly have found, as in the above cases, travesties or imperfect renderings of Egyptian forms. But imitative figures of this kind do not make their appearance, and no attempt has been made to copy even the commonest of the Egyptian characters. Such parallelism as does appear is at most the parallelism of an independent system drawn from a common source. Nor are affinities of this kind by any means confined to Egypt.

Among the closer parallels with the signs of other hieroglyphic systems that it has been possible to indicate, about sixteen (or 20 per cent.) approach Egyptian and an equal number Hittite forms: mere general resemblances, such as those presented by certain figures of fish, birds, &c., being excluded from this rough calculation. Considering that the choice of comparisons is in the case of the Egyptian hieroglyphs very much larger than that of the Hittite, it will be seen that the proportion of affinities distinctly inclines to the Asianic side. Certain signs, such as the wolf's head with the tongue hanging out (No. 44), the he-goat's head (No. 35), the arrow (No. 13), the three-balled spray (No. 54), and Nos. 41, 57, 79 and 80, clearly point to a fundamental relationship between the Hittite and Cretan systems. The double axe moreover is characteristically Asianic, but as certainly not Egyptian. The single axe of the form represented in No. 8 is also non-Egyptian. We are struck too by the absence of the distinctively religious symbols which in Egyptian hieroglyphics are of such constant recurrence. In the Hittite series, on the other hand, as in the Cretan, this hieratic element, though it no doubt exists, does not certainly take up so conspicuous a position.

The somewhat promiscuous way in which the signs are disposed in some of the spaces, notably on Fig. 23b, is strikingly suggestive of the Hittite monuments. When the impressions of the three or four sides of one of the Cretan stones are placed in a row one above the other, as on the analogy of the Babylonian cylinders they would have been in clay impressions, we obtain a columnar arrangement of symbols in relief which curiously recalls the sculptured stones of Hamath or the site of Carchemish. So far more-over as can be gathered from an examination of the Cretan stones, the same boustrophêdon arrangement seems to have been here adopted as on most of the Hittite monuments.[19c]

Yet we have not here, any more than in the Egyptian case, to do with the mere servile imitation of foreign symbols. The common elements that are shared with the Hittite characters are in some respects more striking, and there is greater general sympathy in form and arrangement. The coinci-dences, indeed, are at times of such a kind as to suggest a real affinity. But this relationship is at most of a collateral kind. Some Cretan types present a surprising analogy with the Asianic; on the other hand, many of the most usual of the Hittite symbols are conspicuous by their absence. The parallel-ism, as it seems to me, can best be explained by supposing that both systems had grown up in a more or less conterminous area out of still more primitive pictographic elements. The Cypriote parallels may be accounted for on the same hypothesis.

In the early picture-writing of a region geographically continuous there may well have been originally many common elements, such as we find among the American Indians at the present day; and when, later, on the banks of the Orontes and the highlands of Cappadocia on the one side, or on the Aegean shores on the other, a more formalized 'hieroglyphic' script began independently to develop itself out of these simpler elements, what more natural than that certain features common to both should survive in each? Later intercommunication may have also contributed to preserve this common element. But the symbolic script with which we have here to deal is essen-tially *in situ*. As will be demonstrated in the succeeding section the Cretan system of picture-writing is inseparable from the area dominated by the Mycenaean form of culture. Geographically speaking it belongs to Greece.

§ V.—The Mycenaean Affinities of the Cretan Pictographs.

Some definite evidence as to the chronology of these Cretan seal-stones is afforded by the points of comparison that they offer with Mycenaean forms. Amongst the 'Mycenaean' gems of Crete are found three-sided stones like those represented in Fig. 20*b*.[19d] One of these, a cornelian from the site or neighbourhood of Goulàs, exhibits on one of its sides heart-shaped leaves similar to those seen upon some Mycenaean vases. Vessels with this kind of leaf occurred in the fifth and sixth of the

---

[19c] See p. 301.

[19d] This is in fact an ordinary Mycenaean gem representing apparently a kind of base,

and is inserted on p. 288 merely as an example of form.

Akropolis graves at Mycenae,[20] and it is a common ornament of the stamped glass plaques of the later Mycenaean interments. Another example of this vegetable form may be seen on a low vase found by Professor Petrie in the 'Maket' tomb at Kahun, the approximate date of which is now fixed at about 1450 B.C. by the new evidence supplied by the foundation deposits of Thothmes III. at Koptos.[21] A very similar type of leaf is also seen on a Mycenaean fragment from Tell-el-Amarna, belonging to the age of Akhenaten (Khuenaten) and the early part of the fourteenth century before our era. In a still more literal form, moreover, it appears executed in a brilliant blue on the fresco decoration of the Palace itself.[21a] The leaf on the Goulàs gem presents the distinguishing feature of being decorated with hatched lines;[22] and this peculiarity recurs in an example of the same motive upon one of the vases from the first shaft-grave at Mycenae, the ceramic contents of which, fitting on as they do to some of the types of Thera,[23] must be regarded as earlier rather than later than the Tell-el-Amarna fragments. On these grounds I would approximately refer the Goulàs gem to the fifteenth century B.C.

A more globular variety of the three-sided stones is also represented among Mycenaean gems. On one obtained by me from Central Crete the same leaf-shaped ornament occurs as that described above. On another from Malia, also a cornelian, engraved on two of its faces, are designs of a wild goat struck by an arrow, and of a flying eagle with two zigzag lines proceeding from it—possibly a Mycenaean 'thunder-bird.' An engraved amethyst, again, of this type was found in the Vaphio tomb; and here again we have an indication of date taking us to the middle of the second millennium B.C. and to the most flourishing period of Mycenaean art.

The peculiar form of stone (Fig. 21) with the spirally fluted back,

[20] Schuchhardt, *Schliemann's Excavations*, p. 187, figs. 161—163.

[21] Mr. Petrie in his *Egyptian Bases of Greek History* (*Hell. Journ.* xi. (1890), p. 273) and *Illahun*, &c., pp. 23, 24 had dated this tomb c. 1100 B.C., though he noted as a somewhat incongruous circumstance that the latest scarabs found belonged to Thothmes III. The new comparisons supplied by foundation deposits of Thothmes III. excavated by him at Koptos, such as the ribbed beads, &c., of the same type there found, have now led him however to revise his opinion, and to carry back the date of the Maket tomb to the same time as these deposits. An examination of the Koptos relics, which I had the advantage of making in Mr. Petrie's company, leaves no doubt in my mind that this conclusion must be regarded as final. On other grounds, especially since the discovery of the Tell-el-Amarna fragments, I had already been led to infer that 1100 B.C. was too late a date for the 'Maket' deposit. The existence of the

Thera class of vases would alone be fatal to Mr. Petrie's former view, that the beginning of natural designs on Mycenaean pottery should be brought down so low as this in date. But Mr. Cecil Torr, who in a letter to the *Classical Review* makes much of the inconsistency between the results obtained at Tell-el-Amarna and Mr. Petrie's former opinion as to the date of the Maket tomb, will hardly be gratified to find that the chronological revision that has to be made is in favour of a greater antiquity.

[21a] Specimens of this design presented by Mr. Petrie are now in the Ashmolean Museum.

[22] Petrie, *Tell-el-Amarna*, Pl. XXIX. and cf. p. 17. In this case however the leaf is more lanceolate.

[23] This is notably the case with the vase which bears on its neck two breasts surrounded with dots. Compare Schuchhardt, *op. cit.* fig. 166, p. 189 and Dumont et Chaplain, *Céramique de la Grèce propre*.

which, as pointed out above, seems to originate from a twin Nerita shell type of an earlier period, also occurs among the Mycenaean gems of Crete. One of these, obtained in Candia, is engraved with a typical design of a sepia; another, found at Goulàs, has a combined spiral and vegetable motive of great interest (Fig 42). The leaves in this composition evidently belong

FIG. 42.—GEM, GOULÀS (2 diams.).

to the same water-plant as that seen on a painted ossuary in the form of a hut discovered by Professor Halbherr in a Mycenaean tholos tomb at Anoya Messaritika.[24] The same palmette-like form however recurs in a still more literal guise, occupying the arched interior of the symbol No. 14 on the three-sided stone Fig. 23a. And here an interesting combination suggests itself.

The observation has already been made above that the symbol No. 14 (see below, Fig. 43) which occurs on stones (Fig. 23b, 35c) is the same as No. 15 (Fig. 44), minus the leaf and spirals. I had therefore at first looked upon this latter as a kind of decorative excrescence not essential to the symbol itself. But the symbol in its simplified form, with its arched space below and two curved incisions on the top, remained a puzzle. Judging by the analogy of other signs, it was probably some form of instrument or implement, and the suspicion did cross my mind that it might be connected with house-building and possibly the decoration of ceilings.

But the Goulàs gem places this conjecture in quite a new light. The combination of triquetral curves and vegetable ornament that it presents, at once declares the design to be a part subtracted as it were from a more spacious ornamental surface. The divergent spirals, coupled with foliate or

---

[24] P. Orsi, *Urne Funebri Cretesi*, Pl. I. Perrot, *La Grèce Primitive*, p. 930, quotes with approval a theory of M. Houssay, a zoologist (which he had previously applied to a large cuttle-fish on a Mycenaean vase from Pitanê in the Aeolid), that the ducks, fish and starlike objects seen between the branches of the plant upon the ossuary were supposed to have been generated by it, and that it is in fact the 'barnacle-tree' of folk-lore. For myself however the plant simply represents a water-plant by the side of a stream, the ducks which follow next behind it are flying over the surface of the water, and the fish alone, in the third line, are actually in the water. In fact it is not difficult to trace in this design a reminiscence of a commonplace of Egyptian painted pavements and frescoes, in which river-plants with ducks flying over them or poising on their branches are seen beside a tank or stream containing fish. Only here the forms of the leaves are different from those of the lotos or papyrus seen on the Egyptian models.

floral forms, are the animating principle of a whole series of large decorative compositions, of which the ceiling of Orchomenos is the most conspicuous example in Mycenaean art, but which are in fact the almost literal copies of Egyptian prototypes.

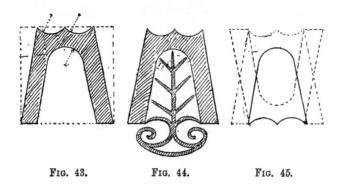

FIG. 43.   FIG. 44.   FIG. 45.

In view of these comparisons it occurred to me that the symbol connected above with the palmette—belonging *ex hypothesi* to a form of Mycenaean ceiling—might have been a simple kind of stencilling plate known as a 'template,' such as is still in use among decorators, and that it was employed for a similar purpose by the artists whose business it was to adorn the palaces of the Mycenaean lords. I accordingly cut out a symmetrical model of the sign (Fig. 43), and made a practical test of its utility in the mechanical procedure necessary for producing such a design. The use of the incurved notches at the top of the figure became at once apparent. The symbol, first applied with the top of the arch uppermost so as to stand on a line ready ruled, gave the upper outline of the leaf, for which the inner margin of the arch supplied the tracing. Now turning the figure upside down, and carefully adjusting its feet to the terminal points of the upper border of the tracing already made, it will be seen (Fig. 45) that the double curves fit into the lower opening of the arch, and give the two incurving lines required for the lower margin of the palmette (Fig. 44).

The form of template suggested by the symbols fulfils the following conditions:—(1) It will be contained in a square, its height being equal to its width. (2) The opening at the base of the arch is equal in width to the space between the exterior horns of the summit. (3) The top of the arch forms a semicircle, the radius of which is equal to that of the curves of the notches at the top.

I.—Now apply the template thus formed to a sloping line *A B* twice on each side of it, as shown in the diagram Fig. 46, so that in all four positions one of its feet rests on the portion *C D* of the said line *A B*.

II.—Apply the template sideways to the sloping line *A B*, as in diagram Fig. 47, and adjust the foot in each case to the lines *E E'*, mark the point of the extreme horns *F F'* and rule the two lines *F G*, *H F*, which are parallels.

Now complete the circular heads of the arches round the points $F F$, which form, in the case given, the centres of the circles thus drawn.

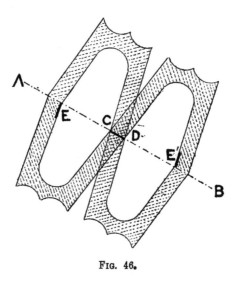

Fɪɢ. 46.

III.—Produce the parallels $F\,G$, $H\,F$ and join the points $F\,F'$. Taking $F\,F'$ as a side, mark off as often as required the same distance on the produced parallels $F\,G$, $H\,F$, drawing at each such distance a fresh parallel to the line

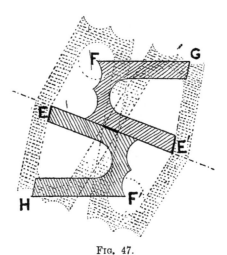

Fɪɢ. 47.

$F\,F'$, and thus producing a series of rhombi. At each of these points repeat the small circles, and to complete the groundwork of this band of the design it is only necessary to draw the curving lines tangentially to them.

The first section of Fig. 48 shows the simple rhombus, the second the same with tangential lines straight and curving. In the third section on the line *A B*, and upon the base *D E* already obtained in Fig. 46, a palmette is formed by reversing the template as in Fig. 46*c*, and so on in the other rhombi. The curving stems and cross lines are then filled in as in the Goulàs gem (Fig. 44), the result being that shown in Pl. XII.

Observation.—In order to fit the design into a square or rectangular surface, as in Pl. XII., each new band of rhombi must be taken back to a starting point (*L*), which must be at the same distance from a right or left margin as was *F* at the commencement.

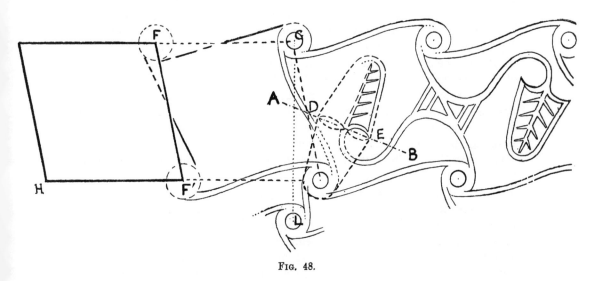

FIG. 48.

The complete design as restored in Plate XII. by the aid of the template symbol may well have decorated the ceiling of a palace hall or princely sepulchral chamber in the great Mycenaean city where the gem was found which suggested this practical application of the pictograph. The typical combination of the volute and vegetable motive which it exhibits affords in turn a secure chronological standpoint. The design before us belongs to the same class as the ceiling of Orchomenos and the fragment of wall-painting from the palace at Tiryns,[25] and was, like them, undoubtedly executed under the immediate influence of the Egyptian style of ceiling decoration that came into vogue under the Eighteenth Dynasty, and the finest examples of which are to be seen in the Theban tombs. The colours on Plate XII. have in fact been supplied from Egyptian analogy.[25a]

---

[25] Schliemann, *Tiryns*, Pl. V.

[25a] The tangential curves of this group of designs are in nearly all cases coloured yellow as if to imitate gold, and this rule also holds good in the case of the wall-painting in the Palace at Tiryns (Schliemann, *Tiryns*, Pl. V.). The alternation of red and blue fields is also common in Egyptian ceilings of this class. I I am indebted to Mr. J. Tylor for some unpublished examples of similar patterns from the

It is probable that at the time when these gems were executed this decorative pattern combining the palmettes and returning curves or spirals was widely prevalent in Crete. The template symbol itself recurs on two seal-stones, in one case with palmette and spirals attached, and on the triangular seal, Fig. 22c, there is a combination of two palmettes and curving lines going in opposite directions, which may be regarded as a simplified version of the fuller motive, as seen in the Goulàs gem. The volute form of the latter stone is, as already shown, characteristic of a class of Cretan gems with purely Mycenaean types, and the connexion that has been established between the design that it presents and Cretan picto-graphic symbols on the one hand, and the Egypto-Mycenaean ceiling decoration on the other, gives us a fresh basis for a chronological equation. The later pictographic class is once more brought into close relation with Mycenaean art, while the Egyptian parallels take us once more to the middle of the second millennium before our era for the approximate date of the seal-stones on which these suggestive forms occur.

In examining the symbols on the Cretan seal-stones various other parallels with Mycenaean forms have already been pointed out. The single figures which occur, such as the young doe or kid in Fig. 24b, the dove pluming its wings on Fig. 31a, fit on both in style and execution to the Mycenaean class. The ship on Fig. 34a and 28a is found again in all its typical lines on lentoid beads of Mycenaean fabric found in Crete. The double axe No. 10, the bent leg No. 5, the bucranium No. 40, all make their appearance as accessories of Mycenaean seals and gems from Pelo-ponnesian tombs. The forms of vases seen in Nos. 28 and 29 are elsewhere held in the hands of Mycenaean daemons, and are the distinguishing types of a whole series of lentoid and amygdaloid gems of Mycenaean character found in Eastern Crete, on the ethnographical importance of which more will be said later on.

It is always possible, as already observed, that some of the smaller objects seen in the field of the typical Mycenaean gems beside the principal design may belong to the same pictographic class as the signs on the angular seal-stones. Such correspondences as those noted above certainly tend to add to this probability. But, bearing in mind the known tendency of the primitive artist to fill up the vacant places of the field with supplementary figures, it does not seem safe to assume that, because small figures identical with the pictographic forms occasionally found their way on to these more decorative objects, they are necessarily to be regarded as having in that position a hieroglyphic value. When however symbols of this character occur in groups, occupying the whole surface of field, the case assumes a different complexion, and it is with this phenomenon that we have to deal in the class of early lentoid gems from Crete represented by Figs. 40 and 41. Of these

ceilings of grottoes near Silsilis, of the Eighteenth and Nineteenth Dynasties. One of these, a series of rhomboidal fields alternately of red and blue, enclosed by yellow tangential curves, affords a close parallel to the Cretan design as restored in Pl. XII.

Fig. 40 exhibits a group of four distinct symbols and part of a fifth, which has unfortunately been broken off. Fig. 41 again contains three signs apparently of the same hieroglyphic character, one of which—the arm holding a curved instrument—resembles the symbol on Fig. 32*b*. These specimens belong apparently to the earlier class of lentoid beads and, like all those of this early class, which in Crete is especially well represented, are cut in soft stone, apparently steatite. One is from Knôsos, the other from the Messarà district of Central Crete, and with them may be grouped another similar lentoid bead from the latter region, with a figure which clearly represents an insular copy of the Egyptian *Ankh*.

§ VI.—The Earlier Classes of Cretan Seal-stones.

THE comparisons already accumulated sufficiently warrant us in referring the most characteristic of the hieroglyphic stones to the great days of Mycenaean art. The connexion established is indeed from many points of view so intimate that it is impossible to avoid the conclusion that there existed within the regions dominated by the Mycenaean culture—in Crete certainly, perhaps in the Peloponnesus—a form of picture-writing of much the same general character as that in use throughout this same period in the 'Hittite' countries of Asia Minor.

But with these Mycenaean comparisons the last word has by no means been said on the origin and evolution of the hieroglyphic forms. There are distinct indications that the beginnings of this picture-writing go back to a far more remote period of Cretan story. Everything tends to show that they are in fact deeply rooted in the soil. The most typical forms of the stones themselves come, as will be seen, of an old indigenous stock. As we go farther back the signs become more pictorial, but they seem still to stand in a personal relation to their owners not to be found on merely decorative gems, and they serve essentially the same purpose as elements of seals.

Of the types described the four-sided equilateral prisms represented by Class II., all of which seem to belong to the Mycenaean period, correspond with an Egyptian form of seal-stone that was in vogue in the time of the Eighteenth Dynasty, and a good specimen of which in green jasper dating from the reign of Thothmes II. (*c.* 1516—1503 B.C.) was found by Mr. Petrie in the Maket Tomb at Kahun. But the three-sided form seems to be a characteristically Cretan product and to go back in the island to a much more remote period.

In the course of my journey through Central and Eastern Crete I came across a series of stones which, though of distinctly earlier fabric, showed the same typical triangular form as Class I. of the later hieroglyphic series. Some of these have the same elongated form, others resemble in shape the more globular variety, but they are larger, and unlike the others, always cut in steatite and never out of harder materials such as cornelian or jasper.

One or two of these earlier types (Figs. 21, 36) have been inserted in the series of hieroglyphic seal-stones already given, as presenting symbols of essentially the same class though at times in a more primitive form and associated with more purely ideographic figures. It would not have been difficult, as will be seen from the contents of the present section, to have added others, and in truth no real lines of demarcation can be laid down between the earlier and the later group. These primitive types show a close correspondence in their designs with certain other classes of early engraved stones found in the island. Amongst these may be mentioned flat disks perforated along their axes and engraved on both faces, button-like stones, and others of truncated pyramidal and sub-conical forms, bored horizontally near the apex.

For the dating of this early group most valuable evidence is supplied by the deposit, already referred to, found at Hagios Onuphrios, near the site of Phaestos, and now preserved in the little Museum of the Syllogos or Literary Society of Candia (Heraklio). This deposit, which contains nothing that can safely be brought down to Mycenaean times proper, is of a homogeneous character, and seems to me to be of capital importance in the history of early Aegean art. Although exact details of the excavation are wanting,[26] it is certain that it represents the remains of early sepulture, dating from the same period as the primitive cemeteries of Amorgos and presenting a series of objects in many respects strikingly similar to those from the Amorgan cists.[26a] Here are the same rude marble idols and vessels, high-spouted clay vases and rude pots with perforated covers, as well as the first beginnings of painted ware, with red, white, and violet stripes on the plain surface of the clay. Here is the square-ended triangular-bladed dagger of the Amorgan graves, the fluted jewelry, but of gold instead of silver; here are the same steatite pendants and spirally ornamented seals. In a word the Phaestos deposit covers precisely the same period as the earlier elements of the Amorgos cemeteries—a period which may be roughly defined as intermediate between the first prehistoric stratum of Troy and the early remains of Thera.[26b] As a matter of fact a two-handled jar with red and white streaks on the blackish-brown ground which must be regarded as one of the latest objects in the Phaestos group approaches in technique some of the earliest ceramic specimens from Thera.

These considerations would alone be sufficient to afford a rough chrono-

---

[26] Professor Halbherr has obligingly collected for me on the spot the following particulars of the find, that are all that are now obtainable. The hill of H. Onuphrios where the objects were found rises opposite the double Akropolis of Phaestos about a quarter of a mile to the North of the ancient city. The find-spot itself was on the southern slope of the hill just above the Khans on the Dibaki road and near the aqueduct of a mill. The deposit was accidentally discovered in 1887 at a small distance beneath the surface. The objects lay in a heap of bones and skulls, but no regular tomb was noted. The whole deposit occupied a space of about four square metres.

[26a] For the early cist-graves of Amorgos see especially F. Dümmler, *Mittheilungen von den Griechischen Inseln* (*Ath. Mitth.* 1886, p. 15 *seqq.* and 209 *seqq.*). The contents of some of the Amorgan tombs, obtained by me in 1893, are now in the Ashmolean Museum.

[26b] For the Hagios Onuphrios deposit see p. 104 *seqq.*

logical guide. The Thera vases may be justly regarded as the earliest examples of the Mycenaean class, which already by the middle of the second millennium B.C. had attained its apogee. On archaeological grounds therefore it would certainly be unsafe to bring down the earliest of the painted vases found beneath the volcanic strata at Santorin and Therasia later than the eighteenth century before our era. On the other hand, the first prehistoric city of Troy must be carried back to a far more remote period. The recent excavations of Dr. Dörpfeld have now made it abundantly clear that the Sixth City on the site of Hissarlik belongs to the great age of Mycenae, or roughly-speaking 1500 B.C.[27] But between this and the once miscalled 'Homeric' City of the second stratum, an interval, estimated by Dr. Dörpfeld in round numbers at 500 years, must be allowed for the intervening settlements, and beyond this again lies the whole duration of the Second City, the beginnings of which go back at a moderate estimate to 2500 B.C. The earliest and most primitive stratum is thus in Dr. Dörpfeld's opinion carried back to the close of the fourth millennium before our era.

But the Phaestos deposit contains direct chronological indications of a kind hitherto unique amidst primitive Aegean finds. Amongst the relics found there occurred in fact a series of Egyptian scarabs belonging to the Twelfth Dynasty and the immediately succeeding period. And happily in this case we have to deal not with cartouches containing names which might possibly have been revived at later periods of Egyptian history, but with a peculiar class of ornament and material that form the distinguishing characteristics of the Egyptian scarabs of Twelfth Dynasty date, and which, though partly maintained during the succeeding Dynasty, give way in later work to other decorative fashions. The amethyst scarabs with a plain face—intended to be covered with a gold plate,—characteristic of this period of Egyptian art, are represented among the Phaestos relics by an example, on which—probably by an indigenous hand,—three circles have subsequently been engraved. A more important specimen however is a steatite scarab engraved below, with a spiral ornament peculiar to this period, to which also in all probability belongs a white steatite bead with a vegetable motive and a scarab with a hieroglyphic inscription. Nor must this occurrence of Twelfth Dynasty scarabs be considered at all exceptional in Crete. From the Messarà district I acquired another of the same class, with a returning spiral ornament of a typical kind; while another scarab found in the same region, with an S-shaped scroll and a cowry-like back, apparently represents an indigenous imitation of a form that came into vogue during the Hyksos period.[28]

---

[27] For the chronology arrived at by Dr. Dörpfeld, see especially *Troja*: 1893, pp. 61 and 86, 87.

[28] This is Professor Petrie's opinion. In his *History of Egypt* (vol. I. p. 208, Fig. 116) are engraved two 'cowroids' of the same character-istic form with cartouches representing blundered copies of the name of Ra-sehoteb-ab of the Thirteenth Dynasty, who reigned about 2510 B C. It is natural to refer these blundered imitations of this cartouche to the succeeding Hyksos Period and with them this 'cowroid'

The Twelfth Dynasty of Egypt is placed by the most recent chronological researches [28a] between the approximate dates 2778 and 2565 B.C. The succeeding Thirteenth Dynasty, which partly preserved the same style comes down on the same reckoning to about 2098 B.C.[28b] With the guide afforded by the presence of these Egyptian relics on the one hand and the approximation to the earliest ceramic types of Thera on the other, we may roughly take the period 2500—1800 B.C. as the time-limits of the Phaestos deposit, which no doubt consisted of successive interments. The generally 'Amorgan' facies of the whole group of objects found quite squares with this result and at the same time prevents us from bringing down the central period of the deposit too near the date of the more developed ceramic style found in Santorin and Therasia. But among the

EGYPTIAN SCARABS XIITH DYNASTY

EARLY CRETAN SEAL-STONES

FIG. 49.

engraved stones found here, together with specimens of other types described above, occurred a typical example of an elongated, three-cornered seal-stone of the earlier class (see below, Fig. 73), having upon it designs of a decorative rather than hieroglyphic character.

Upon a button-like ornament of steatite from the same deposit were engraved three characters of the linear class (Fig. 12); and the remarkable inscribed whorl (Fig. 11), referred to above (p. 284), was found in association with the other relics on the same spot.

---

form. A parallel to this shell-like type is found in the twin *Nerita* bead of the Phaestos deposit, already referred to on p. 289.

[28a] Petrie *op. cit.* p. 147.
[28b] *Op. cit.* p. 204.

The influence of the decorative motives of Twelfth Dynasty scarabs is perceptible upon other early Cretan seal-stones, both of the three-sided and button-like classes. This will be clearly seen by a comparison of the designs of the three scarabs given in Fig. 49*a*, *b*, *c*, with motives taken from the faces of primitive stone 'buttons' and triangular seal-stones of early fabric (Fig. 49*d-h*). It will be seen that the lower part of the ornament on *d* has been 'crossed,' as it were, by the 'broad arrow' symbol which occurs on another facet of the same stone. This and *g* are triangular stones of the same type as that represented in Fig. 19*a*, but of earlier technique than the conventionally pictographic class. The central design on *d* reproduces the principal motive of the scarab above it, and the two signs on *f* are simply incomplete and rude transcriptions of the very characteristic scrolls on *c*.[29] The buttons *e* and *g* were obtained by me from the Messarà district, and the other of a closely similar type (*h*), which is unfortunately broken, is from the Phaestos deposit. It is not too much to say that this

Fig. 50 (enlarged 2 diams.)

taking over of the decorative designs of Twelfth Dynasty scarabs on to these early Cretan stones is of capital importance in the history of European art. In the examples already given will be found simple examples of the borrowing at this early period—*c.* 2500 B.C.—of the returning spiral motive which was afterwards to play such an important part, not in the Aegean countries only, but in the North and West. On the Twelfth Dynasty scarabs this motive, as is well known to Egyptologists, was developed to an extraordinary degree, the whole field being often entirely occupied by divergent spirals to the exclusion of all other elements. These purely spiral types, like the other Twelfth Dynasty motives already noticed, were also copied by the native Cretan engravers. A good instance of this will be seen on another button-like steatite of quatrefoil shape (Fig. 50) from the same Phaestos deposit, exhibiting a series of four divergent spirals.

---

[29] This parallel was kindly supplied me by Mr. Petrie.

From Crete, where we find these Aegean forms in actual juxtaposition with their Egyptian prototypes, we can trace them to the early cemeteries of Amorgos, presenting the same funeral inventory as that of Phaestos, and here and in other Aegean islands like Melos can see them taking before our eyes more elaborate developments.[29a] Reinforced a thousand years later by renewed intimacy of contact between the Aegean peoples and the Egypt of Amenophis III., the same system was to regain a fresh vitality as the principal motive of the Mycenaean goldsmith's work. But though this later influence reacted on Mycenaean art, as can be seen by the Orchomenos ceiling, the root of its spiral decoration is to be found in the earlier 'Aegean' system engrafted long before, in the days of the Twelfth Dynasty. The earliest gold-work as seen in the Akropolis Tombs is the translation into metal of 'Aegean' stone decoration. The spiral design on the Stele of Grave V is little more than a multiplication of that on the Phaestian seal.

In the wake of early commerce the same spiraliform motives were to spread still further afield to the Danubian basin, and thence in turn by the valley of the Elbe to the Amber Coast of the North Sea, there to supply the Scandinavian Bronze Age population with their leading decorative designs. Adopted by the Celtic tribes in the Central European area, they took at a somewhat later date a westerly turn, reached Britain with the invading Belgae, and finally survived in Irish art. The high importance of these Cretan finds is that they at last supply the missing link in this long chain, and demonstrate the historical connexion between the earliest European forms of this spiral motive and the decorative designs of the Twelfth Dynasty Egyptian scarabs.[29b] And it is worthy of remark that in Egypt itself, so far as it is possible to gather from the data at our disposal, this returning spiral system, which can be traced back to the Fourth Dynasty, is throughout the earlier stages of its evolution restricted to scarabs.[29c] The

---

[29a] Compare especially the steatite button-seal from Kuphonisi between Naxos and Amorgos, F. Dümmler (*Ath. Mitth.* 1886. *Beilage* l. l.) : the green marble box from Amorgos (*Op. cit. Beilage* l. Fig. A) and the stone 'pyxis' in the form of a hut from Melos (Perrot et Chipiez, *La Grèce Primitive* p. 910, Fig. 461).

[29b] In the *Hellenic Journal*, Vol. xiii. p. 221, I had already ventured to point out that the early spiral work of the Mycenaean jewels fitted on to that of the earlier stone ornaments of the Aegean islands and the spiral decoration of these in turn to the simple spiral system that attained its apogee in Egypt under the Twelfth and Thirteenth Dynasties. But the 'missing link' to complete the Egyptian connexion was not then in my hands. Dr. Naue, in his recent work, *Die Bronzezeit in Oberbayern* (Munich 1894, pp. 245, 246), while recognizing

that Egypt was the place where this motive first originated, considers that it first reached the Greeks by Phoenician mediation in the fifteenth cent. B.C.—a view which the Cretan and Aegean finds must certainly modify. He considers that it reached Central and Northern Europe through mercantile intercourse due to the amber trade, and apparently favours the view that it came to those regions directly from Egypt. But the early spread of these spiral motives among the Aegean populations affords the most natural explanation. of its first appearance in the Danubian regions. As noticed below, it seems certain that the influence of this Aegean spiral system had begun to leave its mark on Central and Northern European art in prae-Mycenaean times.

[29c] Professor Petrie's observation,

primitive Aegean imitations are also in the same way confined to stonework, and were only at a later date transferred to metal and other materials. The whole weight of the archaeological evidence is thus dead against the generally received theory that the spiral ornament, as it appears on Mycenaean art, originated in metal-work,[29d] though its later application to this and other materials naturally reacted on its subsequent development.

It may be regarded as certain that the early Aegean spiral system born of this very ancient Egyptian contact was beginning to spread in a Northern direction at a date anterior to the great days of Mycenae. At Lengyel in Hungary and at Butmir in Bosnia the spiral decoration appears already on pottery of late neolithic date, and some Hungarian clay stamps with a quadruple spiral design might be taken to be the direct copies of the Cretan steatite seal-stone represented above.[29e] Nor are there wanting indications that the Aegean spiral system was leaving its impress on Italian pottery before the days of Mycenaean contact.

On the present occasion it has been impossible to do more than call attention to the far-reaching importance of this decorative result of the early contact between the Aegean islanders and the Nile Valley in the third millennium before our era. Of that early contact I was able in the course of my Cretan explorations to collect other interesting evidence in the shape of a series of primitive stone vessels of strikingly Egyptian types. In particular, I acquired a stone pot with a cover identical with those found by Professor Petrie in a Twelfth Dynasty deposit at Kahun. It was found beside a skeleton in an early cist-grave at Arvi, on the South-Eastern coast of Crete, in company with other stone vessels, some of a more indigenous character, and a clay suspension vase, very like one from the Phaestos deposit.

The Twelfth Dynasty parallels above instituted are of special value to our present inquiry from the corroboration that they afford to the chrono-

---

[29d] I am informed by Professor Petrie that his researches on this class of scarab lead to this conclusion. An illustrative series of these, including one of Tat-ka-ra of the Fourth Dynasty, has been published by Dr. Naue (*Die Bronzezeit in Oberbayern*, p. 145) from impressions supplied by Mr. Petrie. It would appear, however, that at least as early as the Thirteenth Dynasty this spiral decoration was beginning to spread in Egypt to other objects besides scarabs. There is in the Ashmolean Collection a black-ware vase from Egypt of a style characteristic of Twelfth and Thirteenth Dynasty deposits (cf. Petrie, *Kahun, Gurob and Hawara*, p. 25 and Pl. XXVII. figs. 199–202) which has a punctuated returning spiral ornament running round the upper part of its body. Specimens of similar ware, though without the spiral decoration, were found at Khataneh by M. Naville in company with Thirteenth Dynasty scarabs, in graves deep down below Eighteenth Dynasty accumulations. In Cyprus similar vessels are found in graves anterior, though not long anterior, to the period of Mycenaean influence. Milchhöfer, who like others derived the Mycenaean spiral decoration from wire-work designs (*Die Anfänge der Kunst*, p. 16 *seqq.*), saw a corroboration of this theory in the gold jewelry from the 'Treasures' of Hissarlik (Schliemann, *Ilios*, p. 453 *seqq.*). But many objects from those 'Treasures' do not by any means belong to the remote period to which they were originally referred by Dr. Schliemann. Their whole *facies* shows that they are not far removed in date from Mycenaean times and belong to the Sixth rather than the Second City.

[29e] See especially the Hungarian clay seals represented in the *Compte Rendu du Congrès Préhistorique*, Budapest 1878, Pl. LXX. Fig. 14 and cf. Fig. 13. The S-shaped design so frequent on the Cretan seal-stones is also represented on Fig. 12 of the same series.

logical evidence suggested by the Phaestos deposit. In the one case we have actual association with Egyptian relics belonging to the first half of the third millennium before our era; in the other case we have,—what is even more significant,—unquestionable imitation of the same. Both lines of evidence enable us to refer to this early period some of the more archaic of the three-sided seal-stones and certain types of engraved stone 'buttons.'

But the evidence of the influence of Twelfth Dynasty decorative motives on this group of early Cretan seal-stones, while itself supplying a landmark of extreme antiquity, enables us to carry back to a still earlier date a yet more primitive class of stones still untouched by this Egyptian influence.

Our chief standpoint for this chronological result is supplied by the three-sided stones which of all the forms exhibiting the symbolic figures may be described as the most characteristic.

Setting aside for the moment the most globular variety presenting purely Mycenaean designs, these triangular stones may be divided into the following classes:—

Class I.—Elongated triangular stones presenting groups of symbols or ornaments enclosed in an oval groove somewhat resembling an Egyptian 'cartouche.' Seen at their extremities the central perforation of the stone is surrounded by a triangular groove (*see* Fig. 20*b*, p. 288). The seals of this class are generally of harder materials, such as cornelian, jasper or chalcedony. They present the hieroglyphs in their most conventional form. The materials and some of the designs show that they belong to the Mycenaean Period proper. This class has already been dealt with in Section II.

Class II.—Elongated triangular stones of the same shape as the other with or without the oval groove or cartouche, but of more primitive execution, and of softer material, such as steatite. Both hieroglyphic and linear symbols already occur on some of these, but there is a greater frequency of single designs on the sides, and of purely decorative motives, in some cases derived from Twelfth Dynasty scarabs.

Class III.—Triangular stones of shorter and more compact form (Fig. 51), with or without 'cartouche.' Like Class II. they are of soft materials, such

FIG. 51.

as steatite. S-shaped designs occasionally occur on these, which may possibly be due to Egyptian suggestion, but more elaborate attempts to copy Twelfth Dynasty motives are as yet rare. Human figures, birds and animals, or parts of such, vases and other objects occur, occasionally grouped, and representations of men in various attitudes and employments, but no linear symbols are found. The designs are more pictorial and less conventionalized than in the other groups. This Class seems to overlap Class II., but on the whole is distinctly earlier in style. The subjects represented show a remarkable parallelism with those on certain perforated disk-like stones found in the island. Some of them are very rude and apparently go back beyond the period of Twelfth Dynasty Egyptian influence.

The existence of this most primitive class of triangular seal-stones is of special importance to our subject as showing the indigenous character of the material out of which the later hieroglyphic script was evolved. Many of the subjects, such as the vases, the heads of animals, the birds, branches and

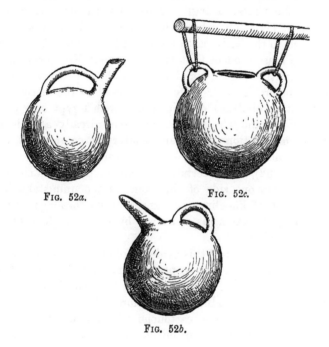

FIG. 52a.

FIG. 52c.

FIG. 52b.

horn-like figures, are essentially the same as those that we find conventionalized and grouped together on the later series. Amongst the ceramic forms we may even see traces of the earlier stages out of which the more advanced types, such as the beaked oenochoê of Mycenaean times, were evolved. These beaked vases take in fact, on some of the stones, the same simple 'askos'-like shapes—betraying their origin from skin vessels—that are characteristic of the earlier strata of Hissarlik and of the most primitive cist-tombs of Amorgos. Others, again, are 'suspension' vases with round bottoms of equally primitive character, and are actually seen hanging from poles. This independent evidence would alone suffice to carry back the early seal-stones of this class to the third millennium before our era. The ceramic forms that they portray, Fig. 52, a, b and c for example, correspond with the round-bottomed types that precede the earliest class of Aegean painted pottery, such as that of Thera or from the Kamares cave in Crete itself.

It will thus be seen that the most typical forms of seals on which the hieroglyphic characters occur, as well as the prototypes of the hieroglyphics themselves, go back on Cretan soil to a very remote period. The earliest class seems, indeed, to have received its characteristic stamp already before the days of that intimate contact with Twelfth Dynasty Egypt which has left its impress on some of the later decorative designs. The evidence collected by Professor Petrie, at Kahun, tends to show that already by the time of Usertesen II., c. 2681—2660 B.C., Aegean foreigners were settled in Egypt. If, therefore, the beginnings of the Twelfth Dynasty Egyptian influences perceptible on the Cretan intaglios date approximately from that epoch, this still earlier class on which this influence is as yet non-apparent may well go back to the early part of the third millenium before our era.

It stands to reason indeed that the indigenous European culture represented by the primitive Cretan population must have reached a comparatively advanced stage before it could have placed itself in the direct contact with the higher Egyptian civilization. Nor was it with Egypt only that the sea-faring enterprise of the Cretan islanders was already at this early date opening up communication—whether predatory or commercial, it might be hard to say. A remarkable piece of evidence is supplied by a seal-stone of the earliest class (Fig. 62), which certainly seems to point to a connexion with the Syrian coast. On one side of this stone is the unmistakable figure of a camel in the act of kneeling, the knees of its fore-legs however being bent in the wrong direction, as if drawn by one who had but a distant knowledge of the animal.

An interesting pendant to this evidence of Oriental intrusion is supplied by a triangular stone, in every respect resembling the early Cretan type, brought back by the late Mr. Greville Chester from the North coast of Syria, and now in the Ashmolean Museum at Oxford. The facets are, in this case, surrounded by the oval groove or cartouche which apparently belongs to the more advanced specimens of the primitive series, but both from its compact form and the rude style of the engraving the stone in question must be referred to the same general period as those grouped above under Class III., and can hardly be brought down later than the approximate date 2000 B.C.

Other independent evidence points to the same early intercourse with Northern Syria. Certain seals in the form of a truncated or obtuse-ended cone occur in Crete, some of which seem also to have been derived at the same early date from this Oriental source. In the Phaestos deposit, above referred to, three of these, and apparently a fragment of a fourth, were found, and it is to be noted as a significant feature that one of these and the fragment were made of ivory. This imported material might in itself warrant the suspicion that this class of seal, which in Crete seems to be of exceptional occurrence, was of foreign origin. As a matter of fact, in Northern Syria, where this must be regarded as a typical form, due no

F

doubt to Babylonian influence, these sub-conical seals are frequently formed of ivory. Seals of this type do not seem to be at home in the intervening Anatolian region, though they are occasionally found there, and their appearance *per saltum* on Cretan soil must be reasonably construed as evidence of an early maritime connexion between the Aegean island and the North Syrian coast. The Hagios Onuphrios find indeed affords a still more irrefragable proof of this contact in a green steatite seal, the upper part of which represents a seated eagle. An exactly similar type from the Haurân is to be seen in the Ashmolean Collection.

Are we therefore to believe that Crete in the third millennium before our era was occupied by a sea-faring race—perhaps Semitic—from the Syrian coast? Such a supposition might explain some of the phenomena with which we have to deal, but in any case it must be allowed that there is a distinctly local character about many of these early Cretan stones. The primitive seal-stones of the triangular form described are, as we have seen, at home in Crete. That their range may have extended to other parts of the Aegean is possible, and an example of a somewhat later type procured at Smyrna by Mr. Greville Chester (Fig. 53) and now in the Ashmolean Collection rather

53a.   53b.   53c.

FIG. 53.

points to some such diffusion, Smyrna being a well-known gathering point of Aegean finds. On the other hand these stones do not seem to be found on the mainland of Asia Minor. Certain three-sided stones of a peculiar ‘gabled-shaped’ class are indeed widely diffused in Cilicia and Cappadocia, but they are as a rule much larger and seem to have no immediate connexion with the Cretan form.[30] The occurrence of a single example of a seal-stone identical both in shape and technique with the most typical Cretan forms on the North Syrian coast is as yet an isolated phenomenon in that region, whereas in Crete itself this form is clearly indigenous and of wide distribution. We have here therefore in all probability to deal with an object brought to the

---

[30] In the case of these stones only one side, which is larger than the others, is engraved, the other two being set at an obtuse angle and forming a sloping back like a gable. ‘Gable-shaped’ may therefore be a convenient term to apply to this well-marked East-Anatolian class, which bears no obvious resemblance to the equilateral stones with which we are concerned. It may yet have a common origin.

Syrian coast from Crete by the same maritime agencies that in the contrary direction brought Syrian forms to the Aegean island.

The materials that my recent researches have enabled me to put together point clearly to the conclusion that the early engraved stones of Crete are in the main of an indigenous and non-Asiatic character. At the outset indeed we are confronted by a negative phenomenon which brings this archaeological result into strong relief. The influence, namely, of Babylonian cylinders is altogether non-apparent. At Melos and Amorgos in deposits of the same age as the early Cretan seal-stones cylinders of native work are found in which the Chaldaean form is at times associated with a decoration which appears to be derived from the Egyptian spiral motives already referred to. On the mainland of Asia Minor again early indigenous imitations of Babylonian cylinders are also widely diffused. In Cyprus they are predominant, and they are very characteristic of the finds along the coast of Syria. It is evident then that a people settling in Crete from that side would have imported this type of seal, and we should expect to be confronted with the same prevalence of the cylindrical type as in Cyprus. But, as has been already observed, this characteristically Asiatic type is at any rate so rare in Crete as to be hitherto unknown among the insular finds. This noteworthy fact seems to exclude the supposition that Crete was occupied by colonists from the Syrian coast at any time during the long period when Syria itself was dominated by Babylonian culture.

We must therefore suppose that if such an occupation took place it was at any rate at an extremely remote period. The parallelism between certain Syrian types and those of Crete is certain. There is moreover a great deal besides in the figures and style of engraving of many of the Cretan stones which strongly recalls other primitive stones found on the easternmost Mediterranean coasts. The early Cretan relics may indeed be said to belong to the same East Mediterranean province of early glyptic design as many similar objects from Syria and Palestine. But, after duly recognizing these undoubted affinities which can to a great extent be explained by the assimilating influences of early commerce, it must nevertheless be allowed that the most characteristic of the early types of Cretan seal-stones are true native products. They are in fact *in situ* geographically. If in the one direction they seem to find parallels *per saltum* on the coasts of Syria and Canaan, in another they fit on to the early engraved stones of Cilicia and the more western part of Anatolia, and they are equally linked on the other side with primitive types of the Aegean islands and the Greek mainland.

Some early forms of seal-stones found in Crete have a much wider diffusion, extending not only to the neighbouring tracts of Asia Minor and the Aegean islands, but still further afield to the West. The button-like stones for example have a very extensive range in Greece and the Levant, they are found in Cyrênê and even appear as imported foreign forms in the Nile valley. These stone buttons may eventually prove to have quite an exceptional interest in the history of Aegean art, as the direct progenitors of the lentoid beads so much affected by the Mycenaean engravers. The most primitive types of the Mycenaean lentoid gems exhibit somewhat conical backs, which may be regarded as a modification of the perforated hump of the typical buttons. The 'buttons' themselves in their original form go back to a much earlier period than the Mycenaean proper, for, as has been shown above, it is upon their decorations that the influence of the Twelfth Dynasty scarab motives is peculiarly apparent.[31]

But these button-like ornaments themselves, with their protuberant perforated backs, what are they but the reproduction in soft stone of proto-types of pinched-up clay? A clay seal of an incurving cylindrical form, but, unlike the Asiatic cylinders, having incised devices at top and bottom and side perforations, was found in the early deposit of Hagios Onuphrios near Phaestos already referred to. And the almost exact reproductions of some of the stone buttons in clay actually occur in the Italian *terremare* and in the Ligurian cave deposits of the neolithic and æneolithic periods (see Fig. 54 *a—c*). The clay 'stamp' from the *terramara* of Montale in the Modenese,

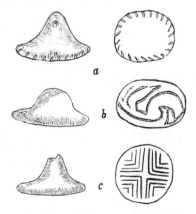

FIG. 54.—CLAY STAMPS FROM EARLY ITALIAN DEPOSITS (reduced to about ½ linear).

a. Pollera Cave, Finale, Liguria (in the Morelli Collection at Genoa).

b. Caverna del Sanguineto, Finale, Liguria. (Cf. A. Issel, *Note paletnologiche sulla collezione del Sig. G. B. Rossi*, Tav. II. 5, 6).

c. Terramara of Montale (in the Parma Museum).

represented in Fig. 54*c*, the top of which, now broken, was probably once perforated, is not only analogous in form, but bears a simple geometrical design almost identical with that on an early steatite 'button-seal' from Knôsos. On the other hand the rudely curving design on *b*, from the Sanguineto Cave in Liguria, strangely recalls the S-shaped designs so usual on the earliest class of triangular seals from Crete (see below Figs. 62, 65).

These terracotta objects, which have sometimes been described as *pinta-*

---

[31] See above, p. 327, Figs. 49 *e, g, h.*

deras [32] from the name given to the clay stamps wherewith the ancient Mexicans painted their bodies, are also found in the early deposits of Hungary [33] and the Lower Danube and reappear in the earliest strata of Hissarlik.

It is not necessary to suppose that these clay stamps on button-seals of Italy and the lands to the North of Greece are of equally early date with some of the Cretan 'buttons.' But they may fairly be taken to show that the clay prototypes of the Aegean seals are European in their affinities. In the West the more primitive clay stamps might well live on to a much later time, while in the Eastern Mediterranean basin the example of Egypt and Chaldaea would naturally promote the substitution of stones—at first of soft and easily engraved materials such as steatite—for the same purpose.

The earlier and simpler series of seal-stones which in Crete precedes the more conventionalized class described in the preceding sections throws a welcome light on the fundamental signification of these later pictographs. The general continuity of ideas is undeniable. The earlier stones to a large extent are of the same triangular type as the later, perforated along their axis and often indeed exhibiting on their several faces somewhat earlier versions of the same designs that reappear among the 'hieroglyphs' of the later class, though in this case single figures, or at most groups of two or three, generally occupy a whole face of the stone.

In a large number of instances taken from stones of this earlier type, gathered by me from various parts of Crete, one side is occupied by a human figure which is evidently intended to represent the owner of the seal. An analogous figure appears on Fig. 36 of the already illustrated series and its frequent recurrence clearly shows that these pictographic stones bore a personal relation to their possessor. Several examples of the more primitive class seem in fact to indicate the quality and pursuits of their owner. On the three-sided stone, Fig. 55, for instance, obtained by me from the site of

55a.   55b.   55c.

FIG. 55.—GREY STEATITE (PRAESOS).

Praesos, the owner was evidently a master of flocks and herds. On one side he appears between a goat and an early form of vessel with handle and spout,

---

[32] A. Issel, *Scavi recenti nella Caverna delle Arene Candide in Liguria*, and see Dr. R. Verneau, *Las pintaderas de gran Canaria*, Ann. p. la Soc. Española de Hist. Nat. xii. 1883.

[33] See above, p. 330, n. 29f. Here a direct Aegean influence seems traceable.

bearing on his shoulders a pole from which are suspended what appear to be four skin-buckets, no doubt intended to contain milk. On the second side he is seen seated on a stool holding in each hand a two-handled vase, and on the third appears a goat—a further allusion to his flocks. In Fig. 56 we see

56a.   56b.   56c.

FIG. 56.—YELLOW STEATITE (BOUGHT AT CANDIA).

on one side a warrior holding a spear, but there appears to have been a more peaceful side to his avocations. On another face is seen a pole with pails of the same kind as those held on to the shoulders of the figure already referred to, and on the third side a goat again makes its appearance. In Fig. 57, again,

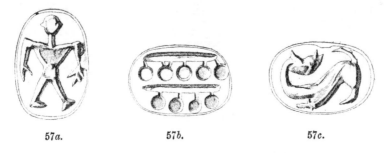

57a.   57b.   57c.

FIG. 57.—BLACK STEATITE (CENTRAL CRETE).

are engraved two poles with vessels of the same kind associated on the other faces with a man and an animal of uncertain species looking backwards, and in Fig. 58 a man is seen in two positions, standing and squatting, accompanied by round-bottomed vessels of primitive Aegean type—notably a kind of *askos* such as is found in the early cemeteries of Amorgos. (See Fig. 52b.)

In Fig. 59a the pole with suspended vessels is brought into immediate connexion with a figure having the limbs and body of a man but apparently either lion-headed or coifed in a lion's scalp. In this case we seem to have the primitive predecessor of the lion-headed human figures of Mycenaean art;[34] the parallelism indeed is of a double nature, for the lion-headed being on this primitive seal-stone is evidently intended to hold the pole with the vessels. Had space allowed he would doubtless have been represented bearing it on his shoulders as in Fig. 55.

58a.   58b.   58c.

FIG. 58.—BROWN STEATITE (CRETE—UNCERTAIN LOCALITY).

But this carrier's function is precisely what is so often found in the case of the mysterious daemons on the later gems, and in the well-known fresco from Mycenae. The association with vessels also reminds us

59a.   59b.   59c.

FIG. 59.—CRETE (BERLIN MUSEUM).

of a familiar attribute of the lion-headed and other kindred beings of Mycenaean times, and in the spouted vases that appear on this same group of early seal-stones we may certainly see the prototypes of those carried by these later daemons.[34] It looks as if in the case of the present stone the place of honour were occupied by some semi-divine protector or mythical ancestor of the actual owner of the seal; and we may trace perhaps a reference to an originally totemic lion of a tribe or family.

On the succeeding face what appears to be the same lion-headed figure is seen standing immediately behind a man in front of whom are two polyp-

---

[34] See on these especially A. B. Cook, *Animal Worship in the Mycenaean Age. J.H.S.* Vol. xiv. (1894), p. 81 *seqq.*

like objects. On the remaining side (59c) there are three fishes. In Fig. 60 a parallel example will be seen of a figure, in this case apparently purely human, raising his hand in the gesture of protection over the head of a man who stands in front of him. The figure in front has his arms lowered in the usual attitude of the personage who seems to represent the owner of the seal. Here too we have the accompaniments of the pole slung with vessels, and the goat.

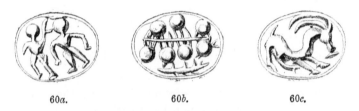

60a.   60b.   60c.

FIG. 60.—DARK STEATITE (CENTRAL CRETE).

Fig. 61 shows on one side a rude two-headed figure in which we must again recognize the prototype of a class of designs which played an important part in the Mycenaean gems of Crete.[35] On the other sides of this stone are some uncertain figures; one seems intended to represent a tall-spouted ewer and a polyp-like object resembling those on Fig. 59 again makes its appearance.

61a.   61b.   61c.

FIG. 61.—BLACK STEATITE (CRETE—UNCERTAIN LOCALITY).

In Fig. 62, already referred to, the owner stands behind a curved design with cross lines, which from Egyptian analogy may perhaps be taken to stand for a walled enclosure. We have here, it may be, a chief in his stronghold, and on another side of the same stone appears a camel, which must certainly be taken to indicate relations of some sort,—not improbably commercial

[35] Cf. for instance the lentoid intaglio found in Crete (Milchhöfer, Anfänge der Kunst, p. 78, Fig. 50 ; Cook op. cit. p. 120, Fig. 15), in which a pair of human legs and a trunk bifurcate into the upper parts of a bull and goat

relations,—with the Syrian coast. The third side here with the S-shaped design, is perhaps merely supplementary or ornamental, as again in Fig. 63,

62a.   62b.   62c.

FIG. 62.—GREYISH YELLOW STEATITE (CRETE)

where the owner is associated on another side with the head of a long-horned ram, a not infrequent feature on these early seals.

63a.   63b.   63c.

FIG. 63.—YELLOW STEATITE (CRETE).

On Fig. 64 the ram's head is seen again associated with a bird and scorpion, the latter a favourite symbol on early Asianic and Syrian seal-stones.

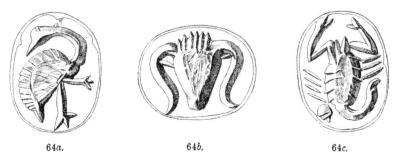

64a.   64b.   64c.

FIG. 64.—YELLOW STEATITE (CRETE).

It seems probable that the long-necked stout-legged bird engraved on this stone is intended for an ostrich, in which case we have another interesting indication of Southern commerce. The intimate contact already at this

early date existing with Egypt makes it not improbable that the trade-route
by which ostriches' eggs—and no doubt their plumes as well—found their
way to Mycenae had its origin in the Aegean enterprise of the third millennium B.C.

In Fig. 65, an S-shaped design, similar to that noticed above, is associated on the remaining sides of the stone with two pairs of pictorial
symbols, in one case two ibexes' heads, in the other apparently a cock and
an uncertain object.   This is the earliest evidence of the cock,—the original
home of which is traditionally sought in Persia,—on European soil.

65a.   65b.   65c.

FIG. 65.—BROWN STEATITE (CENTRAL CRETE).

A commercial purpose is occasionally indicated by a number of incised
dots or pellets which occur beside the figures on these primitive stones, and
which in all cases seem to belong to a duodecimal system.   In Fig. 37 of the
pictographic seals already represented, which might so far as style is concerned have been included in this earlier group, there are seen on one face

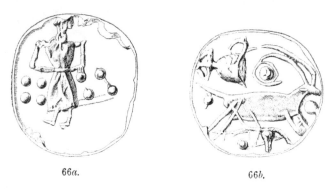

66a.   66b.

FIG. 66.—BROWN STEATITE DISK-BEAD (KAMARES, CRETE).

twelve pellets and on two of the narrower sides of the stone two groups of three.
On a remarkable engraved disk, Fig. 66, obtained by me at Kamares on the
Southern slope of Ida, also of early date, a standing figure clad in a long tunic
appears with four dots on either side of him.   On the other side in the spaces

between the various figures are three dots. On an ivory cone, again, from the Phaestos deposit four similar pellets appear, two on each side of a rude figure of an eagle.

This early duodecimal system is found again on an interesting series of engraved stones, one a seal of curiously Cilician or 'Hittite' type found at Palaeokastro near Baia, opposite the island of Elaphonisi on the Laconian coast, containing a graduated series of similar groups of pellets, first twelve arranged in three rows of four, two seals with six on each, and other small perforated cubes which seem to have stood for units.

The stone Fig. 66 is of great interest as affording one of the earliest examples of a group of pictorial symbols. Round the goat which forms the principal type on one side are three smaller figures—one apparently representing the upper part of an archer in the act of shooting, another a human eye, and below the goat an uncertain object.

In certain cases the figures on these early engraved stones seem to have a reference to some episode in personal or family history. On the green steatite disk Fig. 67, the other face of which is occupied by two goats, a branch, and other objects, we see what, owing to the naiveness of the art, may either be interpreted as a comic or a tragic scene. A figure in a long tunic, behind which is a high-spouted vase, is represented attacking and apparently overthrowing a naked figure seated on a stool.

67a.   67b.

FIG. 67.—GREEN STEATITE DISK-BEAD (CRETE).

Various designs in the primitive series recur in a more conventionalized form in the later class of Cretan seal-stones. On Fig. 68, found near Siteia, are already seen two symbols like the 'broad arrow' of the later hieroglyphic series, and the goat and the skin buckets slung on the pole again make their appearance.

On Fig. 69, what seems to be a ruder version of the same symbol is seen in front of an animal or perhaps a centaur. Then follow on the remaining sides three spearmen and perhaps a dog.

The Twelfth Dynasty influence, as already remarked, is very perceptible

  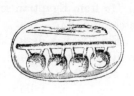

68a.　　　　　　　68b.　　　　　　　68c.

Fig. 68.—Steatite (Found near Siteia, Crete)

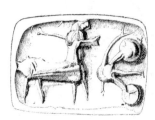  

Fig. 69.—(Crete, Berlin Museum).

70a.　　　　　　　70b.　　　　　　　70c.

Fig. 70.—Green Steatite (Central Crete).

71a.　　　　　　　71b.　　　　　　　71c.

Fig. 71.—Yellow Steatite (Crete).

on some of these early seal-stones. The origin of the designs on Figs. 70a
and 71a from Egyptian scarab motives has already been illustrated by the
sketch on p. 327.

Fig. 72a is a design of decorative character, also probably derived from a
Twelfth Dynasty original, the well-known type, namely, of a scarab with its
face divided into two halves, each containing a divergent spiral pattern.
This design is followed on the remaining sides of the stone by a
rude animal and the head of a bull or ox between two 'swastika'-like
figures and with a branch above.

72a.   72b.   72c.

FIG. 72.—BLACK STEATITE (BOUGHT IN CANDIA).

Fig. 73a may also be traced to the same Egyptian source. Fig. 73b
seems to represent a butterfly—another anticipation of Mycenaean art.

73a.   73b.   73c.

FIG. 73.—STEATITE (CRETE, PHAESTOS DEPOSIT).

The analogies supplied by these earlier classes of Cretan seal-stones are
of fundamental importance to the present inquiry. Some of these more
primitive types are the immediate forerunners of the later 'hieroglyphic'
group, and indeed in their forms and symbolism are hardly distinguishable
from them. What is true of the one must to a large extent be true of the
other, and, as already pointed out,[36] the personal relation in which these earlier
stones clearly stand to their possessor warrants us in believing that the same
holds good of the later class.

---

[36] See pp. 301, 302.

§ VII. THE LINEAR SIGNS AND THEIR RELATION TO THE PICTOGRAPHIC
SERIES.

IT is time to turn from the pictographic series of symbols to the linear
and quasi-alphabetic forms with which they stand in such a close relation.
Evidence has already been brought forward which shows that to a certain
extent both forms of writing overlapped. As already noticed, linear forms
appear on three-sided seal-stones in every respect resembling those which
exhibit the pictographic signs, although on the earliest of these pictographic
seal-stones they do not as yet make their appearance. They occur however
on button-shaped stones belonging to that period of Cretan history which is
marked by the decorative influence of Twelfth Dynasty Egyptian models,
and a stone of this character was found, as already mentioned, in the
Phaestos deposit. That the quasi-alphabetic symbols were employed by the
Mycenaean population in the island is further borne out by a variety of data.
They occur, as we have seen, on the walls of the prehistoric building at
Knôsos, which seems to belong to the same age as the Palaces of Tiryns and
Mycenae or the buildings of the Sixth City of Troy. They are found again
on cups and vases belonging to the same early period, on a Mycenaean
amethyst gem from Knôsos and again on vase-handles found at Mycenae
itself. It is evident therefore that some inscriptions in these linear
characters are as early chronologically as many of the hieroglyphic series,
although, typologically considered, the pictographic group is certainly the
earlier.

The elements at our disposal for the reconstruction of this linear system
may be recapitulated as follows :—

1.—Inscribed seal-stones.

2.—Inscribed steatite pendants and whorls from early Cretan deposits.

3.—The graffiti on vases from Goulàs and Prodromos Botzano and on
the perforated clay pendant from the cave of Idaean Zeus.

4.—Inscribed Mycenaean gem representing a flying eagle, from Knôsos.

5.—The inscribed blocks of the prehistoric building at Knôsos and
another from Phaestos.

6.—The vase-handles from Mycenae and other graffiti on vases from
Mycenaean tombs at Nauplia, Menidi, &c.

7.—The steatite ornament from Siphnos.

From these various sources it is possible to put together thirty-two
different characters (see Table I.) which may be confidently referred to
Mycenaean or still earlier times. But an inspection of the linear signs thus
collected at once reveals striking points of resemblance with those of the
Cypriote and Asianic syllabaries on the one hand, and on the other with the
graffiti signs observed by Professor Petrie on 'Aegean' pottery from
Egyptian deposits at Kahun and Gurob. To these latter I am able to add a

group of linear characters (Fig. 74) on a foot-shaped seal of black steatite obtained by Mr. Greville Chester in Lower Egypt, and now in the Ashmolean Museum at Oxford. The signs on this stone seem to belong to the same system as the Cretan.

FIG. 74.—BLACK STEATITE SEAL (LOWER EGYPT).

The following table of comparisons (I.) shows the Cretan and other Aegean linear forms and the kindred signs of the Cypriote and Egyptian series.

The following are the sources from which the signs indicated in the first and fourth columns of the accompanying Table (I.) are derived.

1.—Seal-stone, Knôsos.
2.—Cretan vases, Goulàs and Prodromos Botzano.
3.—(a) Seal-stone, Province of Siteia. (b) Perforated steatite, Siphnos. A common pictographic symbol is placed in brackets.
4.—Vase, Goulàs. Clay pendant, Cave of Idaean Zeus. Amphora-handle, Tholos tomb, Menidi.
5.—Seal-stone, Praesos.
6.—(a) Steatite whorl, Phaestos; (b) Seal-stone, Praesos.
7.—Seal-stones, Knôsos and Province of Siteia.
8.—Seal-stone, Praesos.
9.—Vase, Goulàs.
10.—Seal-stone, Province of Siteia.
11.—Block of Mycenaean building, Knôsos.
12.—Block of Mycenaean building, Knôsos.
13.—Perforated steatite, Siphnos. Handle of stone-vase, from ruined house, Akropolis, Mycenae.
14.—Vase, Goulàs.
15.—Steatite pendant, early cist-grave, Arbi.
16.—Steatite whorl, Phaestos.
17.—(a) Perforated disk, Knôsos. (b) Early sepulchral deposit, Phaestos.
18.—Seal-stone, Knôsos.
19.—Block of Mycenaean building, Knôsos.
20.—Amethyst intaglio, Mycenaean style, representing eagle: Knôsos.
21.—Whorl, Phaestos.

22.—(*a*) Block of Mycenaean building, Knôsos.   (*b*) Ditto, and also vase, Goulàs.

23.—Perforated steatite, Messarà. Amphora-handle, *Thalamos* tomb, Mycenae.

24.—Mycenaean amethyst (cf. No. 20), Knôsos. Amphora-handle. *Thalamos* tomb, Mycenae.

25.—Mycenaean amethyst (cf. No. 20), Knôsos.

26.—(*a*) Amphora-handle, *Thalamos* tomb, Mycenae (cf. No. 23, 24). (*b*) Block of Mycenaean building, Knôsos.

27.—Handle of stone-vase, from ruined house, Akropolis, Mycenae.

28.—Cretan seal-stone.

29.—Handle of stone-vase, Mycenae (cf. Nos. 13, 27) : partly overlapping a P-like sign.

30.—Perforated steatite, Siphnos (cf. Nos. 3, 13).

31.—Block of Mycenaean building, Knôsos.

32.—Perforated steatite, Siphnos (cf. Nos. 3, 13, 30).

To these may be added the K-like sign on the button-seal (Fig. 13) discovered by Professor Halbherr.

The comparisons instituted in the above table abundantly show that between the Cretan and Mycenaean script, to which the general name 'Aegean' may be conveniently given, and the signs noted by Professor Petrie on the potsherds of Kahun and Gurob there are striking points of agreement. Out of thirty-two Aegean characters no less than twenty are practically identical with those found in Egypt. The parallelism with Cypriote forms is also remarkable, some fifteen of the present series agreeing with letters of the Cypriote syllabary.

That in the case of the Kahun and Gurob signs the proportion should be somewhat larger is only what might have been expected from the relative antiquity of the Egyptian group. As however the evidence on the strength of which Professor Petrie maintains the great age of the foreign signs found on these Egyptian sites has been lately disputed, a few words on the subject will not be out of place.

That here and there some later elements had found their way into the rubbish-heaps of Kahun may be freely admitted without prejudice to the general question of their great antiquity. There seem to me to be good reasons for believing that a few specimens of painted Aegean pottery found belong to a later period than the Twelfth Dynasty. Amongst these fragments are two which are unquestionably of Naukratite fabric. But even of this comparatively small painted class the greater part are of at least Mycenaean date. The most characteristic specimens show in fact points of affinity with a peculiar ceramic class found in Southern Crete and which seems for some time to have held its own there against the more generally diffused Mycenaean types of pottery. Specimens of the class referred to, which in their dark ground colour with applied white and red retain the traditions of some of the earliest Thera ware, have been found in a votive cave near Kamares

TABLE I.

| CRETAN AND AEGEAN LINEAR CHARACTERS | AEGEAN SIGNS FOUND IN EGYPT | CYPRIOTE CHARACTERS | | CRETAN AND AEGEAN LINEAR CHARACTERS | AEGEAN SIGNS FOUND IN EGYPT | CYPRIOTE CHARACTERS |

G

on the southern steeps of Mount Ida, immediately above a Mycenaean nekro-
polis, two of the bee-hive tombs of which I had occasion to visit and in which
Professor Halbherr has now excavated an intact Mycenaean tomb. The above
cave was excavated by Dr. Hazzidaki, the President of the Syllogos or
Literary Society at Candia, and the objects found are now exhibited in the
little Museum of that Society.[36a] My own observations of these have led me
to the conclusion that the ceramic class here represented, though of archaic
aspect, may slightly overlap the more purely Mycenaean pottery in the island.
A spray on one specimen resembles a design on a Mycenaean pot from the
prehistoric Palace at Knôsos ; a fish on another recalls similar forms on the
painted hut-urns from Cretan tholos-tombs, and a barbaric head and arm finds
a close parallel in a painted fragment from tomb 25 of the lower town of
Mycenae. Nos. 1, 6, 7, and 14 and No. 13 of Professor Petrie's Plate of
Aegean pottery show, so far as their shape is concerned, a greater affinity
with this Cretan class than with any hitherto known ceramic group, and the
analogy certainly suggests an early Mycenaean date of some of the Kahun
sherds. Both the Kamares pots and those from Kahun find, on the whole,
their best comparisons with some early types from Tiryns (Schliemann,
Pl. xxiv. c. xxvi*d*. and xxvii*d*.). It may be confidently stated that during
the Aegean period, which roughly corresponds with that of the Twelfth and
Thirteenth Dynasties, and for which the name ' Period of Amorgos ' has
been here suggested—no such finish of ceramic fabric either in form, glaze
or colour as either the vases of Kamares or the fragments from Kahun had
yet been achieved. If then these vessels were imported into Egypt at that
early date they could not have come from the Aegean islands and still less
from the mainland of Greece or from Italy.

But while this, presumably the latest class of pottery found in the Kahun
rubbish-heaps, is for the most part of early Mycenaean date, there seems no
good reason for doubting Mr. Petrie's conclusion that the ruder pottery from
the same deposit exhibiting the incised characters of non-Egyptian forms may
go back in part at least to the days of the Twelfth Dynasty. Isolated
appearances will not mislead the archaeologist as to the general character of
the deposits with which he is dealing, and all their associations point to the
time of the Twelfth Dynasty as the chief period of their formation.[37] At
Gurob again certain of the signs occurred under circumstances which seem
to involve the same early date, while others were found on sherds which
from their character and the position in which they lay belonged as clearly

---

[36a] A paper on the Kamares pottery was read by
Mr. J. L. Myres in the Anthropological Section
of the British Association in 1893. It is to be
hoped that this important study may shortly
see the light in a fuller form. I believe that
my own conclusions as to the date of the pottery agree with those of Mr. Myres.

[37] The special circumstances under which
the signs numbered 141, 21, 125, 126 in Mr.
Petrie's list were found, seem altogether to ex-

clude a later date than that of the Twelfth
Dynasty. Yet these signs belong to the same
class as the others, and occur on pottery of the
same rude fabric which occurs, together with
some of the marks, in foundation deposits of
Usertesen II., and which, in Mr. Petrie's
opinion (*Kahun, Gurob, and Hawara*, p. 43),
' cannot be mistaken for that of any subsequent
age.'

to the days of the Eighteenth Dynasty and to the most flourishing period of Mycenaean culture. So far as the early date of many of these signs is concerned, their extraordinary correspondence with those on the Cretan stones must be regarded as a striking corroboration of Mr. Petrie's views.

Another close parallel to these linear characters and at the same time another proof of their early date has been supplied by the discovery of similar marks on potsherds discovered by Mr. Bliss in the earliest strata

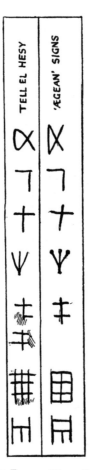

FIG. 75.—SIGNS ON POTSHERDS AT TELL-EL-HESY COMPARED WITH AEGEAN FORMS.

(Cities I. and Sub. 1) at Tell-el-Hesy, which on a variety of evidence are referred by him to a date anterior to 1500 B.C.[37a] The examples given above (Fig. 75) will show that there is something more than a general resemblance

[37a] See F. J. Bliss, *A Mound of Many Cities, or Tell-el-Hesy Excavated*, pp. 21, 23, 25, 28, 29, 30, 33, and 42. These marks on potsherds are described as found exclusively, with the exception of No. 21, in the earliest strata. No. 21 is the last on the list below.

between these marks and the Aegean signs. By including those of Kahun and Gurob the number of parallels may be appreciably increased.[38]

The correspondence of forms in the case of several of the characters found at Kahun and Gurob with those of the Aegean series is in several cases of such a nature as to exclude the supposition of a merely fortuitous resemblance. Few, I imagine, will believe that such a sign as No. 22 was about the same time evolved independently at Gurob, Knôsos and Mycenae.

The same holds good of several of the Cypriote letters. But the Cypriote comparisons are specially valuable since the possibility cannot be excluded that they supply a clue to the actual phonetic value of some of the Aegean characters.

On Table II. I have put together various examples of the Aegean characters which occur in groups of two or more. They are from the following sources:—

1. Vase, Prodromos Botzano (p. 279).
2. Cup, Goulàs (p. 278).
3. Amethyst, Knôsos (p. 281).
4. Seal, Knôsos (p. 293). Signs on two sides, but unfortunately much worn.
5. Seal from Siteia Province (p. 297). On another side ideograph of a man.
6. Block of Mycenaean building, Knôsos (p. 282).
7. Do.
8. Seal, Praesos (p. 293). Signs on two sides, two sprays as pictograph No. 59 on the third.
9. Amphora-handle, Mycenae (p. 273).
10. Handle of stone vessel, Mycenae (p. 273).
11. Button-seal, Phaestos (p. 285).
12. Perforated steatite, Siphnos (p. 287).

To these must be added the Phaestos whorl, Fig. 11b.

The parallels supplied by the Cypriote syllabary suggest the following attempt to transliterate some of these groups:—

1. $//$ · le · lo.
2. $//$ · pa · lo.
3. Ko · sa · ja · ko.
4. E · le.

It remains however uncertain whether the characters should be read from

[38] Where so much still remains to be discovered, it is worth while contemplating at least the possibility that these early signs had also a Western and European extension. In the case of the purely pictographic class, the parallel supplied by the *Maraviglie* in the Maritime Alps has already been cited, to which may now be added another similar group of sculptured signs more recently discovered by Padre Amerano near Finalmarina in Liguria. In connexion with the linear forms I cannot help referring to certain signs on early pottery from the lake-dwellings of Paladru, near Voiron in the Isère, some of which are remarkably suggestive of Aegean parallels. For the pottery see Chantre, *Palafittes du Lac de Paladru*, Album, Pl. X. Figs 1-5 and 7.

left to right or from right to left, neither is it clear where the inscription on the Siphnos stone which presents the largest number of parallels with the Cypriote should begin. Beginning with the sign which as the drawing stands is the topmost on the right, continuing with the lowest and then proceeding

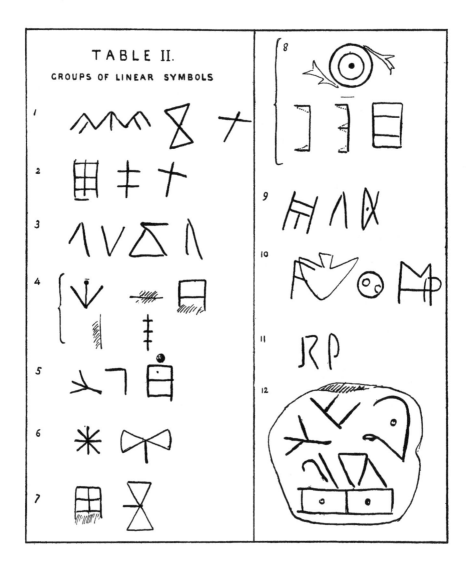

TABLE II.

GROUPS OF LINEAR SYMBOLS

boustrophêdon, the inscription as transliterated by Cypriote letters might read :—

Si · mo · // · no · se · to.

The indications however are too slight to base upon them any too definite conclusions. So far as they go it must be admitted that the phonetic equivalents suggested by the Cypriote parallels seem to belong to a language other than Greek. That we have to deal with a syllabary seems to be clear from the small number of characters contained in the several groups. The close correspondence of this whole series of signs with the Cypriote has already been sufficiently demonstrated. But the very fact that the Cypriote syllabary seems to have been derived from this earlier Aegean and 'Mycenaean' script, or perhaps some parallel Asianic branch, reacts against the Hellenic character of the original. For the Cypriote characters were never originally framed for Greek use. The Greek of the Cypriote inscriptions always seems to be clothed in a foreign dress ill-fitting at the best.

There is indeed the strongest presumption for believing that in Crete at least the race amongst whom the earlier Aegean characters were originally rife was of non-Hellenic stock. It was clearly recognized by the Greeks themselves that the original inhabitants of Crete were 'barbarian' or un-Greek. Herodotos, who brings the Lykians as well as the Kaunians of Karia from Crete, expressly says that the whole of Crete was once occupied by 'barbarians.'[38a] But the most authentic evidence of this non-Hellenic origin is the name of Eteokrêtes or 'true Cretans' applied by the Dorian colonists of the island to the representatives of the indigenous stock, who long continued to live on in the fastnesses of Ida and Dikta. It would even appear that the language of these Cretan aborigines maintained itself in the extreme East of the island to the borders of the historic period. The evidence of this is supplied by an inscription recently found among the ruins of Praesos[39] and now preserved in the Museum of the Syllogos at Candia. This inscription, though written in archaic Greek characters, is composed in a non-Greek language, in this respect recalling the two Lemnian inscriptions, from which however it differs in epigraphy and apparently in language. The following facsimile is from a photograph kindly made for me by Professor Halbherr.

The Praesian stone contains letter-forms in some respects diverging from those of the archaic Greek inscriptions of the island, and in the types of *iôta* and *pi* that are there presented as well as in the early use of Ξ shows a greater approach to Phoenician models. In the concluding letters which form the word *Anait* there seems indeed to be a direct reference to the Semitic Anat or Anaitis, 'the Persian Artemis,' whose image appears on one of the shields found in the cave of the Idaean Zeus.[39a] That at the period when the Praesian inscription was written the indigenous element in the island may have been still largely under Phoenician influence is probable enough, but the inscription itself does not seem to be Semitic.

We may fairly conclude that the language here found represents that of the Eteocretans of whom, as we know, Praesos was a principal stronghold, and it is reasonable to suppose that this was the original language of the

---

[38a] i. 173 τὴν γὰρ Κρήτην εἶχον τὸ παλαιὸν πᾶσαν βάρβαροι.

[39] Comparetti, *Le leggi di Gortyna e le altre Iscrizioni arcaiche Cretesi*, 1893 (*Mon. Ant.* vol. iii.), p. 451 *seqq.*

[39a] F. Halbherr e P. Orsi, *Antichità dell' Antro di Zeus Ideo*, p. 106 *seqq.*, and Atlas Pl. II.; and cf. Comparetti, *loc. cit.* p. 452.

early script with which we are now dealing.   But the materials for comparison are as yet too imperfect on either side to admit of satisfactory results.

In Roman letters the inscription seems to read as follows :— [40]

> ₸ / / N K A L M I T K /
> OS | BARXE | A//₸O
> ARK/APSET | MEG⩘
> ARKRKOKLES | GEP
> /A S E P G N A N A I T

The original is written boustrophêdon, the first, third, and fifth lines running from right to left.   The AI in the last line are in ligature.

It is possible that in the earlier period during which the indigenous Cretan script, both pictographic and linear, seems to have taken its origin the sole or preponderating element is the island may have been the ' Eteocretan.'   It is certain however that at the time when the Homeric poems were composed Crete contained representatives of several other races.   The polyglot character of the island is indeed clearly brought out by the *locus classicus* in the Odyssey.[40a]   The Greek element both Dorian and Achaian is already at home there and seems indeed to have been already of old standing in at least the central district of the island.

But if, at any rate towards the close of the Mycenaean period, there was already a Greek population in Crete, it becomes probable that the mysterious

---

[40] I have followed Comparetti's suggestions *loc. cit.*   [40a] xix. 1. 172 *seqq.*

characters with which we are dealing may also have been used by men of Greek speech.   And from the fact that in Cyprus a similar script, in its origin apparently non-Hellenic, was in use amongst the Greek-speaking inhabitants it becomes in itself not unlikely that the same phenomenon may have occurred in Crete and the Peloponnese where a similar script was in use in much earlier times.   The Greeks of Cyprus spoke a dialect approaching to Arcadian—may they not have taken over with their language a form of writing once in use in the more Western area from which they may be sup-posed to have migrated ?

In view of these possibilities it is worth while examining the grounds of the presumption that the Greek settlement in Crete goes back to Mycenaean times.   In the lines of the Odyssey referred to, which belong to one of the earliest passages preserved to us, Crete is spoken of as the home of several races speaking a variety of tongues, Achaeans and Dorians, Pelasgians, Eteo-krêtes and Kydonians :—

> Κρήτη τις γαῖ' ἔστι μέσῳ ἐνὶ οἴνοπι πόντῳ,
> καλὴ καὶ πίειρα, περίρρυτος· ἐν δ' ἄνθρωποι
> πολλοὶ, ἀπειρέσιοι, καὶ ἐννήκοντα πόληες.
> ἄλλη δ' ἄλλων γλῶσσα μεμιγμένη· ἐν μὲν Ἀχαιοὶ
> ἐν δ' Ἐτεόκρητες μεγαλήτορες, ἐν δὲ Κύδωνες
> Δωριέες τε τριχάϊκες δῖοί τε Πελασγοί.

Here the indigenous Cretan elements are represented by the Eteokrêtes and Kydonians; on the other hand it is evident that the Dorian settlement in Crete at the time when this passage of the Odyssey was composed was of at least sufficiently old standing for the Greek colonists to have assimilated the story of Minôs—set in a Dorian frame.   In the next verses the poet refers to Knôsos, 'the great city,'

> ἔνθα τε Μίνως
> ἐννέωρος βασίλευε Διὸς μεγάλου ὀαριστής,

where, as has been shown by Hoeck,[41] there is a distinct reference to the specially Dorian [41a] time division of nine years or ninety-nine months,—the double Olympiad,—at the end of which 'long year' Minôs according to the tradition used to return to the cave of Zeus to receive fresh instruction and repeat what he had learned before.[42]   But Minôs himself is not Dorian, and the mythical genealogist is content with making the son of the Dorian leader Teutamos, who came from Thessaly to Crete, adopt the children of the

---

[41] *Kreta*, i. p. 246 *seqq.* From the later usage with reference to the election of the Spartan Ephors Hoeck infers that the Dorian kings re-quired a fresh religious sanction for their sove-reignty every nine years, so that they could be said to reign 'nine years.'   He concludes: 'Diess ist unstreitig der tiefere Sinn welcher dem homerischen Μίνως ἐννέωρος βασίλευε unterliegt.   Mag nun immerhin das Wort

ἐννέωρος später in allgemeinerer Bedeutung angewandt seyn, mag selbst schon Homer sich dieses Ausdrucks nicht mit jener bestimmten Rücksicht bedient haben : so lag doch der tiefste grund der Bedeutsamkeit dieser Neun-zahl in jener alten Jahresbestimmung.'

[41a] Dodwell, *de Cycl.* p. 316 *seqq.*

[42] Plato, vi. p. 138.   Cf. Schol. ad *Od.* xix. 178.

Cretan Zeus—Minôs, Rhadamanthys and Sarpedôn.[42a] According to this version we have a Dorian settlement in Crete from the Thessalian Doris, the later Hestiaeotis, under a leader with a Pelasgian name, going back to prae-Minôan times. It is to be observed that this Thessalian connexion fits in with the account of the Odyssey which couples 'divine' Pelasgians and Achaeans with the Dorians in Crete, and with the fact that a son of Minôs bears the name Deukalion. According to the native Eteokretan tradition of the Praesians, preserved by Herodotos,[43] the Greek settlement in Crete had begun before the Trojan war, as a consequence of the depopulation of Crete caused by the disastrous Western expedition that followed the death of Minôs. The Chronicle of Eusebios goes so far as to fix the year 1415 B.C. as the date when the Dorian, Achaean and Pelasgian settlers who had set forth from the country about the Thessalian Olympus landed in Crete.

It will be seen however that though both the native Eteocretan tradition as preserved by the Praesians and the Greek records of the Thessalian expedition assign a great antiquity to the first Dorian settlements in Crete, they are in some respects at variance. The Praesian version speaks vaguely of a first settlement of Greeks and other foreigners in Crete at the time when a large part of it was left uninhabited owing to the wholesale Western exodus that followed the death of Minôs. It then refers to a second depopulation of the island, consequent on the expedition against Troy, followed by a second colonization, which might fit in with the Dorian occupation of the Peloponnese. The Greek account on the other hand plants Dorians Achaeans and Pelasgians in Crete two generations before Minôs, who becomes the adopted son of King Asterios the son of the Dorian leader.

[42a] Diod. iv. 60. In other MSS. of Diodôros the name of the Dorian leader (son of Dôros) appears as *Tektamos*. Andrôn, in Steph. Byz. *s.v.* Δώριον, gives the same version of the Dorian invasion from Thessaly in prae-Minôan times, where the name appears, probably erroneously, as *Teksaphos*. Teutamos, as Hoeck notes (*Kreta*, ii. 1, 24, note 6), recurs in Pelasgian genealogies ; cf. Homer, *Il.* ii. 843.

[43] Her. vii. 171 ἐς δὲ τὴν Κρήτην ἐρημωθεῖσαν, ὡς λέγουσι Πραίσιοι, ἐσοικίζεσθαι ἄλλους τε ἀνθρώπους καὶ μάλιστα Ἕλληνας, τρίτῃ δὲ γενεῇ μετὰ Μίνων τελευτήσαντα γενέσθαι τὰ Τρωϊκά... It is reasonable to bring ἐρημωθεῖσαν into connexion with the failure of the great Cretan expedition to avenge the death of Minôs and the Cretan settlement of Iapygia described in the preceding chapter. The direct reference by Herodotus to Praesian, *i.e.* Eteokretan, tradition in c. 171 gives a special importance to his statement in c. 170 that the Praesians and inhabitants of Polichna, that is the old Kydonians, alone among the Cretans did not take part in the Sicilian expedition. It seems on the one hand to show a recognition of the fact that the Praesians and old Kydonians were of the same stock, on the other hand it does not necessarily mean that Minôan Crete was then in other hands. It is, rather, a patriotic way of accounting for the disappearance of the Eteokretan population from the later Dorian area by the fact that their Western expedition had left the land tenantless, for any one who chose to occupy it. The argument, in fact, runs as follows. The greater part of Crete is occupied by foreigners. These foreigners came in when the original native occupants had gone elsewhere on a Western expedition whence they never returned. But we Praesians, as well as the Polichnites near Kydonia, represent the old inhabitants of the land. Therefore neither we nor they took part in the Western expedition. The survival of the indigenous element in the Kydonian district in the extreme West of Crete supplies a presumption that the Doric colonization of the island did not come by way of Peloponnese. All traditions point to Central—'Minôan'—Crete as the region where Hellenism first took root.

But both traditions are at one in regarding the Dorian occupation of Crete as the result of peaceful settlement rather than of a war of extermination. The account of the ' adoption ' of Minôs by the son of the Dorian chief, after the settlers had seen a second generation grow up on Cretan soil, certainly points to a gradual and bloodless amalgamation of the Hellenic and indigenous elements.

It has been necessary to recall these traditions of the great antiquity of the first Dorian settlement in Crete, since the prevailing tendency is to regard that settlement as a secondary result of the Dorian occupation of the Peloponnese. That the conquest of the Peloponnese may have brought with it a new flow of Dorian migration to Crete is likely enough. The earlier settlements may well leave room for the later attributed to Pollis and Delphos of Amyklae, or for that of Althaemenês from Megara or Argos. The native tradition as represented by the Praesians distinctly points to a fresh Hellenic settlement in the period that succeeded the Trojan war. But to regard the traditions of the early Dorian settlement from Thessaly as given by Andrôn and Strabo as simply fabricated from an erroneous interpretation of the Homeric passage seems quite unwarrantable. The Homeric collocation of Dorians Achaeans and Pelasgians points itself to Thessaly; the name of Deukalion, applied already in the Iliad to a son of Minôs, points in the same direction, and a mere comparison of many of the local names of Crete with Thessalian forms is sufficient to prove an early connexion with that region.[44]

Both tradition, then, and nomenclature favour the view that Greeks and ' Pelasgians ' from Thessaly may have settled in Crete at a date far anterior to that of the Dorian conquest of Peloponnêsos, and it follows that among those who used the curious Cretan script of Mycenaean and earlier times there may well have been men of Hellenic speech.

The archaeological evidence points the same way. Although on the present occasion it is impossible to go into the evidence in detail I may say that my own researches into the prehistoric antiquities of Crete have brought home to me the impression of their great homogeneity. From Kissamos and Kydonia in the extreme West to Praesos and Itanos in the extreme East the same characteristic forms are perpetually recurring. The same type of Mycenaean culture, with certain *nuances* of its own, is common to the whole island. The same rude terracotta images occur throughout, and, as far as our evidence reaches, the funereal rite of enclosing the bones of the dead in painted hut-urns enclosed in *tholoi*, at times excavated out of the rock, was as widely diffused. Diversity of race may have eventually led to some local differentiation. It looks as if the later class of seal-stones with pictographic

---

[44] E.g. *Larissa*, the ancient name for Gortyna according to Steph. Byz. (*s.v.*), *Gortyn* itself comparing with *Gyrtôn* in Perrhaebia (Bechtel, cited by Busolt, *Gr. Gesch.* 1², 330, note); *Phaestos, Phalanna* (cf. too Phalasarna), and *Boebê* are also found both in Crete and Thessaly. *Tritta*, an old name for Knosôs, may possibly be compared with Trikka. There was also a Cretan *Magnêsia*, according to some accounts founded by Magnêtes from Thessaly (Parthen. *Erot.* c. 5). These parallels extend to Macedonia ; compare for instance Olous and Olynthos, Hierapytna and Pydna and the river-names Axos and Axios.

symbols were the special product of the surviving representatives of the aboriginal race in the East of the island, while on the Southern slopes of Ida,— to judge by the relics found in Kamares grotto,—pottery of archaic fabric continued to be produced in early Mycenaean times. Regarding them as a whole however, a great family likeness is perceptible in Cretan remains of this early period ; and, together with the general homogeneity, a remarkable continuity is observable. From about 900 B.C. onwards, to judge from the bronzes of the cave of Zeus, there was a strong Assyrianizing influence, due no doubt to Phoenician contact; but the archaeological break which at Mycenae itself and in the Greek mainland generally is perceptible in the centuries immediately preceding the days of the miscalled ' Archaic' Greek art or, as we should now call it, the Greek art of the ' Early Renaissance,' is in Crete conspicuous by its absence. We have here what may be called late Mycenaean crossed by Oriental influences but still essentially continuous, a phenomenon which repeats itself in an almost identical aspect at Argos and in the Argive relics found at Kameiros. The break caused on the Greek mainland by the intrusion of a geometrical style of art fitting on to that of the Danubian valley and the Hallstatt culture of Central Europe is reasonably connected with a tide of invasion from the North, of which the Dorian invasion of the Peloponnese represents the southernmost wave. But the Dorian invaders who are supposed to have been hurried on to Crete by the same migrating impulse—where have they left their mark on Cretan antiquities ? Certain geometrical elements came in no doubt, fibulae are found identical with those of the Dipylon or the Boeotian cemeteries, but the evolution of Cretan art is still in the main continuous. That there was at this period a fresh Dorian colonization of parts of Crete is probable : but the new comers were merged in the body of Dorian inhabitants already long settled in the island, and received from them the artistic traditions that they had themselves handed down from Mycenaean times. And in architecture at least, let it be remembered, it was the Dorian element that was to represent the true Mycenaean tradition.

Another piece of archaeological evidence completely disposes of any difficulty that might be felt as to a colonization of Crete from such a comparatively distant quarter as Thessaly in Mycenaean times. Mycenaean culture was early planted in the Thessalian coastlands, as appears from the tombs of that period discovered on the headland opposite Volo, the ancient Iolkos.[45] But, among the vases found in these Thessalian tombs, is a peculiar class of one-handled pots displaying water-plants with arrowlike or cordiform leaves and waved lines below, apparently indicative of water. A vase of the same form but with a different ornamentation was found in Akropolis Grave No. III. at Mycenae,[46] but in the Maket tomb at Kahun, now shown by Mr. Petrie to belong to Thothmes III.'s time,[47] there was deposited a

[45] See Wolters, *Mykenische Vasen aus dem nördlichen Griechenland,* *Athen. Mitth.* xiv. (1889) p. 262 *seqq.*
[46] A leaf ornament of the same character occurs on a vase from Grave I. and another from Grave VI., as well as on a glass paste ornament from Grave III.
[47] See above, p. 318.

pot not only of the same shape as the Thessalian examples but with an identical design. Iolkos and the Nile Valley were thus either in direct commercial connexion, or at any rate supplied from the same source, as early as the fifteenth century B.C., and it cannot be doubted that Crete, lying between the two formed an important link in the chain. The vegetable motive described is indeed a characteristic feature on Cretan gems of the Mycenaean period [48] and will doubtless be eventually found to have played an important part in Cretan ceramics. The archaeological evidence makes it well-nigh certain that there was a direct intercourse between Crete and the famous Thessalian port at the period when, according to tradition, the first Dorian colonists along with Achaeans and Pelasgians found their way to the island from that very quarter.

There are therefore good grounds for supposing that the Greek colonization in Crete goes back well into the period during which the primitive forms of script with which we are dealing were in general use in the island. As a matter of fact the later epigraphic monuments of more than one of the Dorian cities of Crete actually exhibit what appear to be survivals of some of the characters belonging to the prae-Phoenician script with which we are now dealing. Professor Halbherr has made to me the valuable suggestion that some of the characters brought to light by the present investigation had influenced the forms of certain letters that occur in the most archaic Greek inscriptions found in the island, while in other cases they seem actually to have survived as marks of division. Thus at Lyttos there is seen a form of O consisting of two concentric circles, with or without a central dot,[49] identical with the symbol No. 2d of the pictographic series or 28 of the linear. At Eleutherna [50] and Oaxos [51] there is found a form of Vau ⋏ which suggests a differentiation from the Phoenician Vau under the influence of the linear character No. 20 Ⅹ On the other hand the double axe symbol 𐄂 occurs both at Gortyna [52] and Lyttos [53] as a mark of division.[54]

But in considering the possibility that this early script may have been made use of by men of Greek speech we cannot restrict our survey to Crete alone. The indications that we possess, at any rate in the case of the linear characters, point to a much wider diffusion, Mycenaean in its most comprehensive sense. The early script that we find in Crete extends, as we have seen, to the Peloponnese, but quite apart from this phenomenon there is abundant evidence to show that the Mycenaean culture in the two areas, at least in its earlier stages, was singularly uniform in aspect. On this occasion it is impossible to enter into details, but it may be sufficient to say that the engraved Mycenaean gems found in Crete show a remarkable correspondence with those from Mycenae itself, the Vaphio tomb and other Peloponne-

---

[48] See above, p. 323.

[49] Comparetti, *Leggi di Gortyna, &c.*, p. 201.

[50] *Op. cit.* p. 418, Inscr. 194, l. 6.

[51] *Op. cit.* p. 402, Inscr. 187, l. 3.

[52] *Op. cit.* p. 117, col. ix. l. 43. In the note it is spoken of as 'un segno insignificante.' It is used to separate two very different clauses.

[53] *Op. cit.* p. 434, Inscr. No. 203, l. 7. In this case the sign is written horizontally instead of vertically.

[54] At Corinth the same sign is used for E, in Pamphylia for Ξ.

sian sites. The art of the Vaphio gold vases finds itself an absolute counterpart on a fragment of a stone vessel presenting similar reliefs obtained by
me on the site of Knôsos. The cult-scenes on the gold rings find their
nearest pendant on a Cretan example. A bronze figure of the same early
type as that found at Tiryns, and another from Mycenae, has lately been discovered in a cave near Sybrita. In short, whichever way we look, we see
Mycenaean art in Crete as it now begins to emerge before us displaying the
same typical form that it bears in Peloponnêsos. And few will be found to
doubt that, whatever may have been the nationality of the dominant race in
whose hands both in Crete and Peloponnesos this art first took its characteristic shape, in Peloponnesos at any rate it was taken over by Greek-speaking
tribes. The close relation with Crete into which the royal house of Mycenae
is brought in the Iliad and in Greek tradition generally [55] becomes in this
connexion of special interest. Atreus himself or his son Pleisthenês marries
Aëropê the granddaughter of Minôs, who in turn becomes the mother of
Agamemnôn and Menelaos. Idomeneus, the uncle of these, is the guest of
the Argive princes—notably of Menelaos—and connected with them in the
affairs of peace as well as war.[56] According to local sagas Agamemnôn
himself founded the Cretan Mykênae [57] and other cities of the island. There
are besides this a considerable number of local names common to Crete and
the Peloponnese,[58] but some at least of these may be due to the later wave of
Dorian migration from Laconia and the Argolid.

The early connexion between Crete and other parts of the Greek
mainland, notably with Attica and Boeotia, is borne out by the same evidence
of tradition and nomenclature. In the case of Boeotia indeed it is tempting
to see in the peculiar form of the Ⴀ a trace of the influence of the linear
or pictographic symbol resembling a four-barred gate.

Incomplete then as our evidence still is, it tends to show that the use
of early script with which we are dealing may have been shared both on
the mainland and in Crete itself by men of Greek speech. The data at
our disposal seem to warrant the conclusion that the diffusion of this early
system of writing was in fact conterminous with that of the Mycenaean form
of culture. The pictographic class of seal-stones seems to have been princi-
pally at home in Crete. But the linear script had evidently a very wide
range. In Crete itself the linear characters occur on a greater variety of
materials than the more pictorial forms. In the Peloponnese they are found
not only at Mycenae itself but at Nauplia, they reappear at Menidi and at
Siphnos, and in Egypt they are found on the early potsherds of Kahun
and Gurob. On the early whorls of Hissarlik we already see traces of
similar signs.[58b] In Cyprus we find a closely allied system, which had also
diffused itself along the coastlands of Asia Minor, surviving into classical
times. It further appears that very similar signs had invaded the coast of

---

[55] See especially Hoeck, *Kreta*, ii. p. 397, seqq.

[56] *Il.* iv. 256 *seqq.*, and cf. *Il.* iii. 230 *seqq.*

[57] Vell. Paterc. i. 1.

[58] E.g. *Amykla, Therapnae, Pharae, Boiae, Tegea, Arkades, Lampê* (or Lappa). Cf. Busolt, *Gr. Geschichte*, 2nd ed. p. 329 *seqq.*

[58b] Sayce in *Ilios*, p. 691 *scqq.*

Canaan. There can be no doubt that many of the marks referred to above as found on the potsherds of Tell-el-Hesy, which has been identified with the ancient Lachish, belong to the same system as the linear characters of the Aegean and Egyptian deposits. May we suppose that both in this case and at Kahun and Gurob these marks were originally derived from a Cretan or Aegean source? The appearance in the later strata at Tell-el-Hesy of Aegean painted pottery, including a fragment representing a bird which resembles one from the sixth Akropolis tomb at Mycenae, certainly points to an influence from this side.

The evidence as a whole reveals a very direct relation between the linear forms and the Mycenaean form of culture in its most typical shape. On the Goulàs cup, the Knôsos amethyst, the prehistoric walls of the same site, the vase-handles of Mycenae itself, it appears on objects of the characteristically Mycenaean class. In short there seems every reason to believe that this quasi-alphabetic group of signs represents the typical form of Mycenaean script.

The pictographic series on the other hand may be regarded as more local in distribution and as the special property of the indigenous Cretan stock, who appear to have continued to use this less developed form of picture-writing at a time when their neighbours had generally adopted what may be a more simplified form of script. To this pictographic or hieroglyphic group I would provisionally give the name of 'Eteocretan.' That it lived on in Crete into Mycenaean times is proved by a variety of evidence and that it belonged to a people largely under Mycenaean influence is also clear enough. But it does not seem to have been so widely current amongst the Aegean peoples of the Mycenaean age as the linear system.

In comparing the two groups the first question that naturally suggests itself is: How far does the pictographic or 'Eteocretan' series represent the parent stock out of which the linear or 'Mycenaean' system proper may be supposed to have been evolved?

That there is a connexion between the two systems is certain. Not only do both groups of characters occur on seal-stones of the same typical form, but in some cases the linear forms are seen accompanied by signs belonging to the hieroglyphic class. On the four-sided stone Fig. 36, two facets of which are occupied by purely ornamental designs, we find the two remaining sides occupied respectively by a figure of a man, which may be taken to have an ideographic signification, and a group of three linear signs. On the triangular seal-stone Fig. 29 we see another group of three linear characters preceded by a sign which represents a simplification of the eye-symbol that recurs on several stones of the purely hieroglyphic series, and on the remaining side two other pictographic characters. On Fig. 30 two sides are filled with linear characters, while the third exhibits what is possibly a rude version of the hippocamp symbol. Moreover on the stone vase-handle from Mycenae we see the quasi-alphabetic forms accompanied by a more pictorial representation which closely resembles an early form of the 'broad arrow' symbol as seen on some of the Cretan stones. It is a noteworthy fact that a similar mixed usage of pictographs and alphabetic forms occurs on early Sabaean inscriptions. Thus on two Sabaean gravestones a pair of eyes appear above the inscription.[59] In another case a bull's head, a pictographic rendering of the personal name Taur, appears at the beginning of the inscription.[60] In Greek archaeology this combined usage of letters and symbol is curiously illustrated by the signatures of magistrates and officials, which are often reduplicated in the same way.[61]

This mixed usage is a clear proof of the overlapping of the two classes of script with which we are now dealing. Abundant evidence indeed has been already accumulated that at any rate in the Eastern part of Crete the pictographic signs continued to be used by a people in other respects under the full influence of Mycenaean culture.

Again several of the signs that take their place in the pictographic series are themselves practically linear. Among these may be mentioned the concentric circles (No. 2d, e), the loop (No. 80), the S and X-shaped forms, the gate or shutter and some forms of the ' broad arrow.'

This tendency to linearization perceptible in the hieroglyphic series might by itself suggest the possibility that we had here the prototypes of quasi-alphabetic forms. I had even, as already observed, set to work to simplify and reduce to linear shape the pictographic symbols that occurred on the first seal-stones that came under my notice before I was yet acquainted with the linear class. More limited as was then my material the results thus experimentally arrived at led me to the conclusion that the Cretan hieroglyphs might eventually prove to supply the origin of a system of script closely approaching the syllabaries used in Cyprus and parts of Anatolia at a later date.

It was therefore the more satisfactory to find this *a priori* supposition confirmed by the subsequent discovery in Crete itself of an independent linear system of writing containing in several cases forms corresponding to the simplified versions of the hieroglyphs that I had already worked out.

Of course it is not to be expected that all or even a large proportion of types represented in any given pictographic or hieroglyphic system should recur in a series of alphabetic or syllabic characters derived from it. The pictographic method of writing necessarily involves the use of a very large number of signs, while on the other hand an alphabet or syllabary can only be arrived at by a rigorous system of limitation and selection. Out of the seventy odd 'hieroglyphic' signs from the Cretan stones—a number which will no doubt be largely increased by future discoveries—it would not be reasonable to expect more than a limited set of correspondences with the linear forms, especially when it is borne in mind that of this linear system too we have as yet probably little more than a fragment before us.

The correspondences that do occur between the two systems are nevertheless of so striking a kind as to warrant us in believing that there is a real

---

[59] Glaser, *Mittheilungen über einige aus meiner Sammlung stammende Sabäische Inschriften, &c.*, pp. 304 and 326.

[60] *Op. cit.* p. 325.

[61] See above, p. 273.

relationship. In instituting the comparisons below the pictographic signs referred to have been taken from the somewhat advanced types represented on the Mycenaean seal-stones of Eastern Crete. But inasmuch as the linear forms overlap this conventionalized pictorial class and go back themselves, as already shown, to a very early date, it would not be literally true to say that they are derived from pictographs in the stage represented by these 'Eteo-cretan' seals. The actual prototypes of the linear forms would probably have been pictographs of a ruder 'graffito' and almost linear type themselves, such as we find on some of the most archaic Cretan stones and on the whorls of the earliest settlements at Hissarlik. But, these allowances being made, the later pictorial series of which alone we have a fairly copious record seems in certain cases to supply a probable clue to the origin of the linear signs.

In instituting the comparisons between the pictographic and linear signs as sketched in the annexed diagram (Table III.) it has been found useful to introduce a certain number of Cypriote forms as supplementing the Aegean types at present known to us. But, in addition to this, the parallels presented by the linearized pictographs to Semitic letter-forms are in several cases so striking that I have not hesitated to include these in the table of comparisons. There have been also added certain Greek letters either of uncertain origin, like the ψ, or presenting forms like the Boeotian four-barred E or the Cretan O with a concentric circle,[62] which apparently go back to prototypes earlier than any existing Semitic models. In the case of Zayin I have even had recourse to the Sabaean form as very probably in this case representing the completer shape of the letter. These Semitic comparisons recall certain parallels presented by some of the linear Aegean signs included in Table I. Nos. 10, 24, and 25 of the series there represented much resemble forms of *Gimel* and *Lamed*, while No. 14 suggests a reduplicated *Yod*.

The annexed table of comparisons both in its general bearing on the origin of Aegean and possibly Cypriote letters from pictographic originals and in the special parallels that it supplies to Semitic forms must certainly be taken to throw a suggestive light on the vexed question of the origin of the Phoenician alphabet. If it once can be shown that in Crete and the Aegean coastlands a primitive system of picture-writing gave birth to a linear syllabary akin to that of Cyprus, the possibility that the Phoenician forms may after all have had a non-Egyptian origin becomes distinctly greater. If in this Aegean region an ox's head or a fence or tree assumed linear forms practically identical with those that bear the names of the same or similar objects in the Phoenician series, what good reason is there for supposing that the same phenomenon may not have repeated itself in other parts of the same East Mediterranean basin?

Some of the parallels with Semitic names and forms, as will be seen from the following examples, are altogether startling.

On the remarkable perforated disk (Fig. 11) from the Phaestos deposit a rude and elongated figure of a horned animal—apparently a bull or ox—

---

[62] See p. 360.

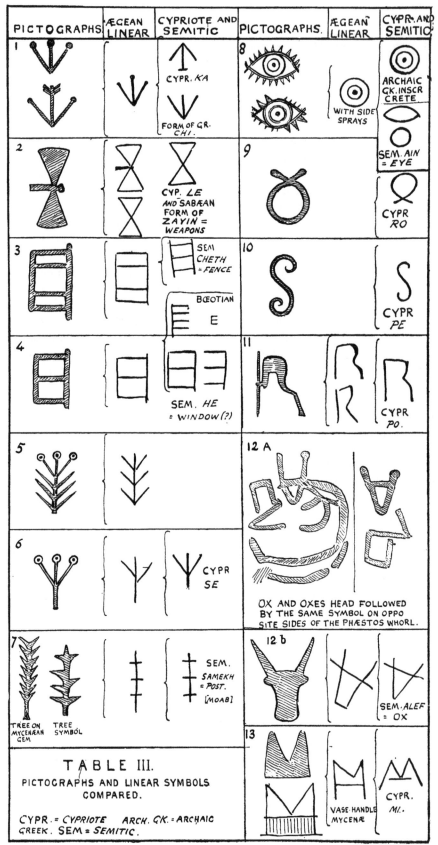

PICTOGRAPHS	ÆGEAN LINEAR	CYPRIOTE AND SEMITIC	PICTOGRAPHS.	ÆGEAN LINEAR	CYPR. AND SEMITIC
1		CYPR. KA / FORM OF GR. CHI.	8	WITH SIDE SPRAYS	ARCHAIC GK. INSCR CRETE / SEM. AIN = EYE
2		CYP. LE AND SABÆAN FORM OF ZAYIN = WEAPONS	9		CYPR RO
3		SEM CHETH = FENCE / BŒOTIAN E	10		CYPR PE
4		SEM. HE = WINDOW (?)	11		CYPR PO.
5			12 A		
6		CYPR SE	OX AND OXES HEAD FOLLOWED BY THE SAME SYMBOL ON OPPOSITE SIDES OF THE PHÆSTOS WHORL.		
7 TREE ON MYCENÆAN GEM / TREE SYMBOL		SEM. SAMEKH = POST. [MOAB]	12 b		SEM. ALEF = OX
TABLE III. PICTOGRAPHS AND LINEAR SYMBOLS COMPARED. CYPR. = CYPRIOTE ARCH. GK. = ARCHAIC GREEK. SEM = SEMITIC.			13	VASE HANDLE MYCENÆ	CYPR MI.

H

appears in conjunction with a linear symbol **◘✔**. On the other side of the same stone the head of the same animal like an ∀ upside down is followed by the same symbol **◘✔**. The A is thus brought into direct connexion with the bull or ox. On a seal-stone again (Fig. 26*a*) we find a pictorial representation of an ox's head accompanied by other symbols, while on the pendant from Arbi (Fig. 16) occurs what seems to be a linear form of the same, standing by itself. It cannot be doubted that the A symbol of the Cretan series is derived from an ox's head. If we turn to Phoenicia we find the same symbol with a record of its pictographic original in its name *Alef* = an ox. According to De Rougé's theory however, which still holds the field, we are asked to believe that in Phoenicia the symbol, notwithstanding its name, was derived from the hieratic representation of an eagle.

In Crete we see the double axe linearized into a symbol **Ⴟ**, like a closed X or two crossed Z's. From the occurrence of this symbol as equivalent to Z on the Sabaean inscriptions there seem to be good reasons for believing that the original Semitic form of *Zayin* was of this shape, and *Zayin* is generally translated 'weapons,' which would find its natural explanation in the pictograph of the double axe. But the received derivation is from the hieratic sketch of a flying duck. The Cretan pictograph for a tree is reduced to the same form as the Phoenician *Samekh* = a post, the origin of which is by De Rougé's theory traced to the hieratic degradation of an Egyptian chair-back. The two Cretan pictographs which may stand for a gate, fence, or shutter and the accompanying linear forms are practically identical with the Semitic *Cheth* = 'a fence' and *He*,[63] supposed to mean a window.[64] Here again form and name correspond in both cases, but we are asked to believe that the Phoenician forms are descended respectively from a sieve and a maeander. The eye is one of the commonest of the Cretan pictographs, and the Phoenician *Ain*, signifying 'an eye,' for which even De Rougé's ingenuity failed to discover an Egyptian prototype, is the natural linearization of a similar form.

The Cypriote system, as we have seen, seems to fit on to the Cretan and 'Aegean.' But if we examine the Cypriote syllabary we are struck in the same way with the close parallelism of many of the forms with those of the Phoenician alphabet. These resemblances have been accounted for by a supposed process of assimilation due to the preponderating influence of the Semitic forms. But now that it is becoming clear that the Cypriote syllabary represents a branch of a very much older system, which appears in Crete, the Peloponnese and elsewhere long before we have any record of Phoenician writing, the ground is cut away from any such theory.

The matter seems at first sight to be complicated by the fact that the Cypriote characters that bear the greatest resemblance to Phoenician forms have in all cases a different phonetic value. The sign which answers to *He* in the Semitic series reappears in Cypriote as equivalent to *ri*. In the same way *Tau* becomes *lo*, *Gimel*, *ko*, and *Yod*, *ni*.

But these phonetic divergences can be accounted for by a very simple

---

[63] The Boeotian E with four bars, introduced in the Plate, rather points to an older form of

He resembling the pictograph No. 4.

[64] See Isaac Taylor, *The Alphabet*, p. 171.

supposition—which may indeed be now regarded as something more than a mere theoretic possibility. Supposing that throughout a considerable part of the East Mediterranean basin a pictographic system of communication had grown up analogous in its earliest stage to the picture-writing in use among the North American Indians, such pictorial signs would have had, as they still have amongst savage races at the present day, a currency beyond the limit of individual languages. The signs would in fact have been ideographic and independent of language. But as the system became more conventionalized and developed and finally gave birth to a kind of linear shorthand of the original picture-writing, the figures which had stood for individual objects and ideas would in due course acquire a shortened phonetic value representing syllables and letters. And, as a necessary consequence of this process, these signs, though they may have been derived from what was originally a widely current pictorial stock, would now take the phonetic values imposed by the language spoken by individual tribes. The old picture of an ox or an ox's head would have been generally intelligible. But reduced to the linear stage the ox's head might be an A in one country and a B in another.

It looks as if some process of this kind had actually occurred on the coasts and islands of the Aegean and the further Mediterranean shores. The Cretan pictographs give us a good warrant for believing—what even without such evidence common sense would lead us to expect—that a primitive system of picture-writing had existed in the Aegean lands at a very remote period. The antiquity of these figures is indeed in some cases curiously brought out by the fact already pointed out, that they actually exhibit the actions of a primitive gesture-language. Furthermore we see certain ideographic forms no doubt once widely intelligible on the coasts and islands of the Eastern Mediterranean reduced to linear signs which find close parallels in Cyprus and Phoenicia. Finally, some of the names of the Phoenician letters lead us back to the same pictographic originals which in Crete we find actually existing.

To the Phoenicians belongs the credit of having finally perfected this system and reduced it to a purely alphabetic shape. Their acquaintance with the various forms of Egyptian writing no doubt assisted them in this final development. Thus it happened that it was from a Semitic source and under a Semitic guise that the Greeks received their alphabet in later days. But the evidence now accumulated from Cretan soil seems at least to warrant the suspicion that the earlier elements out of which the Phoenician system was finally evolved were largely shared by the primitive inhabitants of Hellas itself. So far indeed as the evidence at our disposal goes, the original centre of this system of writing should be sought nearer Crete than Southern Syria. The natural script of the Semites was the cuneiform, derived from their ancient contact with Chaldaea, and which, as we know from the Tell-el-Amarna tablets and other sources, was still the dominant script of Syria and Palestine at a time when 'Minoan' Crete and Mycenaean Greece had, as we have seen, already evolved independent systems of writing both pictographic and linear.

H 2

In view of these facts it is at least worth while to weigh the possibility that the rudiments of the Phoenician writing may after all have come in part at least from the Aegean side. The more the relics of Mycenaean culture are revealed to us the more we see how far ahead of their neighbours on the Canaanite coasts the Aegean population then was in arts and civilization. The spread of their commerce led them to seek plantations in the Nile Valley and the Mediterranean outlets of the Arabian and Red Sea trade. The position was the reverse of that which meets our eye at a later date. It was not Sidon that was then planting mercantile settlements on the coasts and islands of Greece. Those were the days when Philistine Askalon weighed heavily on Sidon herself;[65] when the Viking swarms from the Aegean isles and the neighbouring coastlands were a thorn in the side of the Egypt of Thothmes III.[66] and his successors. But the relics of Aegean civilization now brought to light at Tell-el-Amarna and the Fayoum, like those found at Lachish, show that there was another besides the purely piratical side to the expeditions of these maritime races. Barbaric invasion and migration followed as usual the routes of more peaceful commerce, and, as in the case of the Northmen, the Viking period of the Aegean peoples was succeeded, at least as early as the twelfth century B.C., by a period of fixed settlement of which the name of Palestine, the land of the Philistines, is the abiding historic landmark.

In considering the possible influence of the early Aegean script on the Semitic races, the colonization of the Southern coasts of Canaan by the Philistines and their kin is of primary importance. The commercial instinct of the invaders is well brought out by the occupation of Gaza, lying on the trunk-line of commerce between Syria and the Nile Valley and forming at the same time the Mediterranean goal of the South Arabian trade-route.[67] The Southern district in which Gaza lay seems to have been the special possession of the Cherethites,[68] who at times give their name to the whole Philistine confederation—a name which in the Septuagint version of Ezekiel [69] and Zephaniah [70] is translated by Κρῆτες. Gaza itself bore the title of Minôa [71] and according to Stephanus was the legendary foundation of Minôs and his brothers. Its chief god Marnas was identified with Zeus Krêtagenês.[72] The central district of Philistia seems to have been occupied by the tribe from whose name that of the Philistines was itself in all probability derived, the Pulasati [73] 'from the middle of the sea' who played such a prominent

---

[65] Cf. Justin xviii. 3.

[66] On a stêlê at Karnak Thothmes III. is made to show his majesty to the Danônas of the Isles 'as a lion that sleeps upon the carcases.' This implies that the Danônas were already molesting the coasts of Egypt. The Maket tomb (see above, p. 318) and other archaeological sources give evidence of more peaceful contact between Egypt and the Aegean peoples in the early reigns of the Eighteenth Dynasty.

[67] On the importance of Gaza in the ancient geography of Palestine see especially G. A. Smith, *Historical Geography of the Holy Land*, p. 181 *sqq.* As 'the natural outpost across the desert from Egypt' it played the same part that Damascus did with reference to Assyria.

[68] I. Sam. xxx. 14.

[69] C. xxv. 16.

[70] C. ii. 5.

[71] Steph. Byz. *s.v.* Μινώα.

[72] Steph. Byz. *s.v.* Γάζα ; cf. Hoeck, *Kreta*, ii. 369. The name *Marnas* was erroneously brought into connexion with the Cretan *Martis* = Maiden, which appears in Britomartis.

[73] See W. Max Müller, *Asien und Europa nach altägyptischen Denkmälern*, 1893, p. 389.

part in the invasions of Egypt under Ramses III. and Merenptah, and whose name when brought into connexion with that of the Cretans curiously recalls the δῖοι Πελασγοί,[74] so early settled in the island side by side with ᾽Ετεό-κρητες, Achaians—probably the Akayvas of the same Egyptian monuments—and Dorians. Another member of this group of Aegean and West Anatolian peoples whose maritime enterprise was now a terror to Egypt and its border-lands was the Takkara,—*ex hypothesi* Teucri, the eponymus of whose race whether he appears at Salamis or Troy is doubly connected with Crete.

These people are brought into close connexion with the Pulasati and Danônas (presumably Danai) in the expeditions against Egypt, and from an interesting notice in the Golenischeff Papyrus[75] it appears that Dore or Dor on the coast of Canaan was already by about 1100 B.C. known as a city of the Takkaras. In Greek legend this city was founded by ' Dôros the son of Poseidôn '[76] and its inhabitants were known as Δωριεῖς.[77] The names are certainly suggestive, and in days when Ionians and probably Achaians were already mentioned in Egyptian records a trace of a Dorian element on these shores hardly need surprise us. That among the various elements from the Aegean coastlands who took part in the Philistine Confederation men of Greek stock may already have found a place as early as the twelfth or eleventh century B.C. can no longer at least be regarded as an improbable hypothesis. It is perhaps not without some actual warrant in fact that in the Septuagint version of Isaiah[78] the Philistines themselves are translated by ῞Ελληνες.

Hebrew tradition is unanimous in bringing the Philistines from the ' Isle of Kaphtor.' ' Island ' here may simply mean distant coasts such as those of the Aegean in general, but the alternative form of Cherethim applied to the same people certainly indicates that, in so far as it stands for an island, Kaphtor should be applied to Crete rather than Cyprus. This consideration lends an additional interest to the suggestion that Kaphtor may be connected with Keftô, whence came the people who of all those represented on Egyptian monuments most clearly show Mycenaean characteristics. Their costume, their peaked shoes and leggings, the dressing of the hair, the characteristic vessels they are represented as bearing to Thothmes III., show the closest parallels with Mycenaean forms. This parallelism, as shown by the Pelo-ponnesian remains such as the wall-paintings of Mycenae, the shape and ornament of the gold cups and vases and notably the figures on the Vaphio cups, has already been pointed out.[79] The identification of the Kefti with the

---

[74] Chabas, who transliterates ' Pulasati ' as ' Pelestas,' had already identified them with the Pelasgians in his *Antiquité his-torique.* So too Renan (*Histoire générale des langues sémitiques,* I[4], p. 53): ' Une hy-pothèse très vraisemblable, adoptée par les meil-leurs exégètes et ethnographes, fait venir les Philistins de Crète. Le nom seul de Plishti... rappelle celui des Pélasges.' This view also commends itself to Maspéro (*Hist. Anc. des peuples d'Orient,* p. 312). W. Max Müller (*op. cit.* p. 368), while admitting the possibility that the Pulasati are Philistines, rejects the

view that they are Pelasgians. But he accepts the identification of the Shardin, Turshas, Akayvas, and Jevanas, with Sardinians, Tyrseni, Achaians, and Ionians.

[75] W. Max Müller, *Asien und Europa nach altägyptischen Denkmälern,* p. 388.

[76] Steph. Byz. *s.v.* Δῶρος.

[77] Steph. Byz. *l.c.* Παυσανίας δὲ ἐν τῇ τῆς πατρίδος αὐτοῦ κτίσει Δωριεῖς αὐτοὺς καλεῖ

[78] C. ix. 12.

[79] This comparison, first instituted by Puch-stein, has been further brought out by Stein-dorff, *Archäologischer Anzeiger,* 1892, p. 12 *seqq*

Phoenicians has been further shown to rest on a confusion of Ptolemaic times.[80] The ruddy hue of the Kefti chiefs in the Theban paintings,—which seems to be the Egyptian way of rendering the rosy European cheeks,[81]—as well as their dress and facial type are clearly non-Semitic.

Isolated resemblances such as those presented by the bronze figure from Latakia, the Syrian Laodicea, now in the Louvre,[82] or by the details of some Hittite or early Cilician reliefs cannot weigh against the much greater conformity with Mycenaean types, and, to the Peloponnesian examples already cited, my own researches now enable me to add a striking array of Cretan parallels. Here it may be sufficient to say that throughout Eastern and Central Crete the commonest types of Mycenaean gems show as their principal designs a series of vessels evidently representing originals in the precious metals, some with beaked spouts, some with S-shaped double handles and slender bases which reproduce several of the most characteristic types of the vessels offered by the Kefti chiefs to Thothmes III. on the Theban tombs. The men of the Vaphio cups, who present such a striking resemblance to the Kefti tributaries as seen in the walls of the Rekhmara tomb, recur with the same flowing locks on a fragment of a stone vessel from Knôsos. It is true that, if on the one hand the Keftô folk are brought into connexion with the people 'of the islands of the sea,'[83] on the other hand they are found in the company of Hittites and of men of Kadesh and Tunep (Daphnê) and the Upper Rutenu of Inner Palestine. But if, as there is good reason for believing, the carrying trade of the East Mediterranean was at this time largely in Mycenaean hands, these associations and perhaps the tribute of silver and copper—it may be from Cilicia and Cyprus—that the Kefti bore in addition to their artistic vases would be accounted for without difficulty. The matter will appear even simpler if we may accept the view that the name of Keftô is to be identified with that of the Caphtor[85] whose inhabitants included both the Aegean islands and the coast of Canaan in their

---

[80] In the Canopus Decree 'Kefti' is translated Φοινίκη, which led Ebers and other Egyptologists to accept the identification of the Kefti with Phoenicians. W. Max Müller however (*Asien und Europa nach altägyptischen Denkmälern*, p. 337) has shown how valueless the Ptolemaic tradition was in such matters. From the place in which the name appears—after Naharin and Heta—in early Egyptian lists, he himself concludes that it represents Cilicia. Steindorff, who also (*op. cit.* p. 15) rejects the identification with Phoenicia, is led to seek the Kefti in the Gulf of Issos or Cyprus. But, as noticed above, the archaeological evidence does not favour either Cilicia or Cyprus. Cyprus, as we know, was touched by Mycenaean culture in comparatively late times, but it was never, certainly, a centre of its propagation. The early Mycenaean spiral work, such as is seen on the Kefti vases, is foreign to Cypriote remains. On the Cicilian mainland Mycenaean traces altogether fail us. The

numerous engraved stones found there, like others recently brought back by Mr. D. G. Hogarth from Ain-Tab in Commagene, are of Hittite and non-Mycenaean character.

[81] *Op. cit.* p. 351.

[82] Longperier, *Musée Napoléon*, 21 ; Perrot et Chipiez, *Phénicie, &c.*, 429, 430.

[83] In the Rekhmara inscription.

[84] Tomb of Men-Kheper-ra-seneb, *Mission archéologique française au Caire*, 5, 11, and cf. W. Max Müller, *op. cit.* p. 347, and Steindorff, *loc. cit.*

[85] Ebers' suggestion that Caphtor = '*Kaftvere*' or Great Keftô (which he assumed on the strength of the Canopus decree to be Phoenicia) is rejected by W. Max Müller (*op. cit.* p. 390), who however expresses the opinion that the name Keftô has nevertheless a real connexion with Caphtor : 'Ist der Name Keftô (the orthography approved by him, p. 337) auszusprechen so ist allerdings der Anklang mehr als zufällig.'

field of activity. The later confusion of their land with Phoenicia in the Canopus Decree is in this connexion not without its significance.

In considering the question of possible Philistine influence on the origin of the Semitic script it must always be borne in mind that the actual colonization of Palestine is only a comparatively late episode in a connexion which goes back to far earlier times. The parallels supplied by the more primitive class of Cretan seal-stones abundantly show that there was a lively intercourse between the Aegean island and the Easternmost Mediterranean coast as early as the third millennium before our era. Aegean enterprise, according to Mr. Petrie's researches, penetrated at an equally early date into Egypt, and of this again we have now the counter-proof in the Twelfth Dynasty Egyptian relics found in Cretan interments. Whether or not a 'proto-Semitic' element may have existed in Crete itself and other parts of the Aegean world from very early times is a question beyond our present scope. Should this prove to have been the case it might simplify some problems that are at present enigmatic. There certainly seems to be a deeply-lying community of early tradition between Crete and the Semitic world older than can be accounted for by Phoenician agencies of post-Mycenaean times. A river-name like Iardanos, Minôs the Cretan Moses, Diktynna in some respects so closely akin to Derkê and Atargatis, the evidence supplied by Mycenaean relics of the early cult of Astarte, are only a few of a series of suggestive indications. There are Thraco-Phrygian elements no doubt which must be set off against these, but the possibility that the later colonization of Canaan by the Philistines and their allies was in part at least a return wave of Europeanized Semites cannot be altogether ignored.

Conjecture apart, however, the evidence accumulated by the present inquiry may be fairly taken to establish certain fixed points in the early archaeology of Crete and the Aegean lands. Proofs have been given of the existence of a pictographic system of writing which in Eastern Crete at any rate survived into Mycenaean times, but the earlier stages of which, on the evidence of Cretan seal-stones, may be traced far back into the third millennium before our era. The pictographic system of Crete is itself of independent growth and, though perhaps modified by Egyptian influences, is not a mere copy of Egyptian forms. In the Aegean world it occupies the same position as is occupied by the 'Hittite' hieroglyphs in Asia Minor or Northern Syria, and it must in all probability be regarded as a sister system with distinct points of affinity and perhaps shading off into the other by intermediate phases. The pictorial forms are intimately connected with a system of linear signs which also goes back to a high antiquity, but which in certain cases at least may be referred with some confidence to a pictographic origin. These linear signs are of wide Aegean range, they fit on to the syllabaries of Anatolia and Cyprus and show besides many striking points of affinity with Semitic letters. They are found in Egypt at an early date in the wake of Aegean influences and seem to have been the common property of the Mycenaean civilization.

In all this we have an interesting corroboration of an ancient Cretan tradition recorded by Diodôros. According to the Cretan version the received account of the invention of letters by the Phoenicians was only partially true. The Phoenicians had not invented written characters but had simply 'changed their shapes.'[87] In other words they had not done more than improve on an existing system,—which is precisely what the evidence now before us seems to suggest. We may further infer from the Cretan contention recorded by Diodôros that the Cretans themselves claimed to have been in possession of a system of writing before the introduction of the Phoenician alphabet. The present discovery on Cretan soil of both a pictographic and a linear script dating from times anterior to any known Phoenician contact thus affords an interesting corroboration of this little regarded record of an ancient writer.

But the evidence of the Cretan seal-stones to which these remarkable results are mainly due does not end here. In many other ways they throw a new and welcome light on the early culture of the Hellenic world. The implements and instruments of Crete in Mycenaean times are here before us. The elements are present for the reconstruction in one case at least of a great decorative design. The pursuits of the possessors of the seals are clearly indicated, the ships that they sailed in, the primitive lyres to which they sang, the domestic animals that they tended, the game that they hunted, the duodecimal numeration that they employed. On the earlier seals we are able to trace the beginnings of this Aegean culture to an age much more remote than the great days of Mycenae. We see before us the prototypes of more than one of the characteristic forms of Mycenaean times. Here are its familiar vases in an earlier stage of development, its decorative beads approaching more and more the primitive clay button, its butterflies and polyps and even its mysterious lion-headed beings. Above all we find abundant proofs of a close contact with the Egypt of the Twelfth Dynasty, and of the taking over of the spiral system that characterizes the scarab decoration of that period. We can thus, as already pointed out, trace to its transported germ the origin of that spiral system which was afterwards to play such an important part not in Mycenaean art alone but in that of a vast European zone. On the other side we find at this same early period, which may be roughly characterized as the middle of the third millennium before our era, accumulated proof of a close connexion with the Easternmost Mediterranean shores. The camel, perhaps the ostrich, was already familiar to the Cretan merchants and the ivory seals of Canaan were hung from their wrists. Already at that remote period Crete was performing her allotted part as the stepping-stone of Continents.

---

[87] Diod. Lib. v. c. 74. φασὶ (sc. οἱ Κρῆτες) τοὺς Φοίνικας οὐκ ἐξ ἀρχῆς εὑρεῖν ἀλλὰ τοὺς τύπους τῶν γραμμάτων μεταθεῖναι μόνον. M. J. P. Six kindly reminded me of this passage. He adds 'la découverte des hiéroglyphes préhelléniques en Crete est venue bien heureusement confirmer ces données des anciens, qui, on le voit, en savaient bien plus sur les temps préhelléniques qu'on ne le croit communément.'

THE SEPULCHRAL DEPOSIT OF HAGIOS ONUPHRIOS

NEAR PHAESTOS

IN ITS RELATION TO PRIMITIVE CRETAN AND AEGEAN

CULTURE.

THE SEPULCHRAL DEPOSIT OF HAGIOS ONUPHRIOS NEAR PHAESTOS IN ITS RELATION TO PRIMITIVE CRETAN AND AEGEAN CULTURE.

THE Phaestos deposit so frequently referred to in the preceding pages[1] is of such unique importance in the early archaeology of Crete and the Aegean shores that a more detailed account of some of the objects found there will not be out of place. The objects were found in a heap of human bones and skulls at a spot on the hill of Hagios Onuphrios, which rises about a quarter of a mile to the North of the double Akropolis of Phaestos. The find-spot, as already noticed, was on the Southern slope of the hill just above the Khans on the Dibaki road, and near the aqueduct of a mill. The deposit itself belongs to the period of Aegean culture so well illustrated by the early cemeteries of Amorgos, and to which the epithet 'Amorgan' may perhaps be conveniently applied. It represents a series of interments probably covering a considerable space of time, but the latest objects found, such as the painted vases (Figs. 106—108) below, are still prae-Mycenaean in their character, though showing some approximation to the earliest ceramic style of Thera. The deposit is in fact a part of what was evidently a prehistoric Necropolis of Phaestos.

Among the seal-stones found in this deposit a three-sided steatite of the early type has been already engraved on p. 345 (Fig. 73), and the influence of a Twelfth Dynasty Egyptian motive has been traced in part of the design. Another quatrefoil seal is given in Fig. 50 (p. 328) showing a fully-developed spiral motive fitting on to the early Egyptian class. Several Egyptian scarabs referred by experts to the same period were discovered. Amongst these is a characteristic type of amethyst, though this, like the white steatite (Fig. 77), is ornamented with plain circles. A more elaborate decoration into which the spiral largely enters is seen in Fig. 78. Fig. 79 is a steatite bead-seal, perhaps suggested by a form of shell, and is somewhat analogous to the class described as 'cowroids,' while Fig. 80, with a similar leaf ornament, is carved above into a convoluted relief which has been compared to two nerita shells with a common whorl.[2]

The clay cylinder (Fig. 81) with side perforations is remarkable. Unlike the Babylonian cylinders, it is engraved only at top and bottom. The design above may perhaps be interpreted by the light of a better example of a similar design on an early seal from the Heraeon at Argos[3] as a man standing before a large shield approaching the typical Mycenaean form.

---

[1] See p. 14 (283) and 56 (325) *seqq.*
[2] See p. 20 (289).
[3] For the sight of an impression of this I am

indebted to Dr. Waldstein, Director of the excavations of the American School at the Heraeon.

Fig. 77.—White Steatite Scarab
(2 diams.).

Fig. 78.—Steatite Scarab
(2 diams.).

79a.

79b.   79c.

Fig. 79.—Steatite (2 diams.).

80a.   80b.

Fig. 80.—Steatite (2 diams.).

81a.   81b.   81c.

FIG. 81.—TERRACOTTA (Natural Size).

82a.   82b.   83a, b.

FIG. 82.—STEATITE (2 diams.).   FIG. 83.—STEATITE, HAURÂN.

81 (bis) a.   FIG. 81 (bis).—DARK STEATITE (2 diams.).   81 (bis) b.

84a.   FIG. 84.—STEATITE (2 diams.).   84b.

Of the button-seals, one with what look like rude linear characters has been engraved on p. 16 (285), Fig. 12.   A broken specimen of another (Fig. 81 *bis*) exhibits part of a curved design, the Twelfth Dynasty origin of which has been illustrated above.[4]   The most remarkable for form is the eagle-shaped seal (Fig. 82) of green steatite, engraved below with a very rude figure of a goat.   This seal, as already pointed out,[5] finds a close parallel in a Syrian

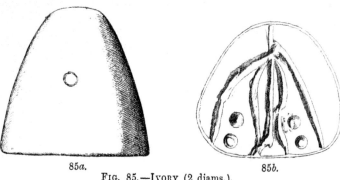

85*a*.   85*b*.
FIG. 85.—IVORY (2 diams.).

example from the Haurân, which is here illustrated (Fig. 83 *a, b*) for the sake of comparison.   The Haurân seal is engraved with curious characters. Equally Oriental in their connexions are a class of conical and sub-conical seals, represented in the Phaestos deposit by four examples.   Fig. 84 *a, b* is of steatite, and the interlaced design appears to be of Egyptian derivation.   The other three are of ivory, a material which, as already

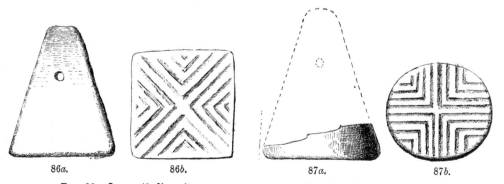

86*a*.   86*b*.   87*a*.   87*b*.
FIG. 86.—IVORY (2 diams.).   FIG. 87.—IVORY (2 diams.).

noticed (p. 64 (333)), is not unfrequently used for seals of the same form from the coast of Syria.   Fig. 85 appears to represent a rude figure of an eagle with two pellets on either side.   The geometrical designs on Figs. 86, 87 recur on the Maeonian mould and a curious leaden object to be described below.[5a]   Among other small stone objects are a yellow steatite

---

[4] See p. 58 (327), Fig. 49*h*.   [5] P. 65 (334).   [5a] See p. 132, 133.

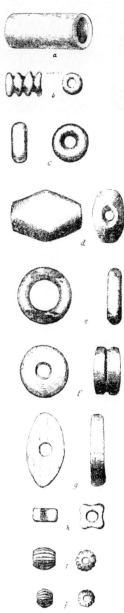

pendant which recalls a similar class of objects from the early cist-graves of Amorgos (Fig. 88), and some cylindrical heads of marble and steatite. Other types of beads from this deposit of various materials, steatite, rock-crystal, variegated limestone, and gold, are given in Fig. 89 *a—j*. It is of course conceivable, considering the circumstances of the Hagios Onuphrius find, that some one or other of these smaller objects like the beads may have got down from a higher level. But wherever it is possible to judge of the date of relics contained in this deposit their prae-Mycenaean character is well marked and there is every probability that these minuter objects belong to the same period.

Among the jewels are a quartz crystal worn as a pendant with a gold mounting (Fig. 90), a small spiral band of gold (Fig. 91), and the small gold objects represented in Figs. 92, 93, the application of which is indeterminate. The granulated work of Fig. 94, which may have served as the end of a pin, is interesting from its occurrence on some of the jewelry found at Hissarlik.[6] It recurs on Mycenaean gold-work.

In some cases a bronze core has been plated over with gold. This method is followed in the case of three curious objects, two of which are engraved in Figs. 95, 96, and again of Fig. 97, perhaps part of a hilt, and three perfected knobs (Fig. 98). The fluting of the thin gold plate with which this latter is covered somewhat recalls the spirally fluted silver beads of an Amorgos grave. The objects represented in Figs. 95, 96, of which another (96 *bis*) occurred wholly formed of steatite, may perhaps be compared with a perforated instrument of diorite found in the burnt city at Hissarlik.[7]

Among the jewelry may be perhaps classed a miniature figure of a beaked vase carefully wrought in variegated limestone (Fig. 99), and another, less well shaped, of black steatite. These objects seem to have been pendants serving as amulets. As an ornamental appendage vases of similar form adorn the top of a gold pin[8] found in one of the three smaller treasures of Hissarlik.

FIG. 89 (Natural Size).— *a.* Marble and Steatite ; *b.* Dark Steatite ; *c.* Rock-crystal ; *d.* Dark Steatite ; *e.* Limestone ; *f.* Steatite ; *g.* Ivory ; *h.* Dark Steatite ; *i.*, *j.* Gold.

---

[6] Cf. especially the gold earring, Schliemann, *Ilios*, p. 489, Fig. 840.   [7] *Ilios*, Fig. 557, p. 440.

[8] Schliemann, *Ilios*, p. 488, Fig. 834, and cf. Fig. 850.

FIG. 88.—YELLOW STEA-
TITE (Natural Size).

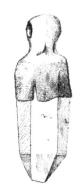

FIG. 90.—CRYSTAL WITH GOLD
MOUNTING (Natural Size).

FIG. 91.—GOLD
(Natural Size).

FIG. 92.—GOLD
(Slightly Enlarged).

FIG. 93.—GOLD
(Slightly Enlarged).

FIG. 94.—GOLD
(Natural Size).

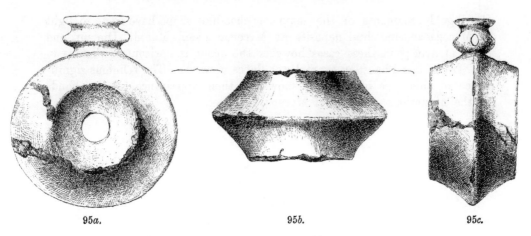

95a.   95b.   95c.

FIG. 95.—BRONZE, GOLD-PLATED (Natural Size).

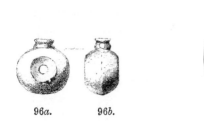

96a.   96b.

FIG. 96.—BRONZE, GOLD-PLATED
(Natural Size).

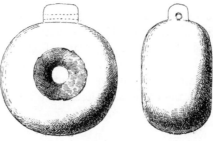

FIG. 96 bis.—STEATITE.
(Natural Size).

FIG. 97.—BRONZE, GOLD-PLATED
(Natural Size).

FIG. 98.—BRONZE, GOLD-PLATED
(Natural Size).

Small gold ornaments of the same oenochoê-like shape have come to light in Mycenaean sepulchral deposits at Mycenae itself, Menidi, Dimeni, and again at Arnê;[9] in these cases however the spout is horizontal, whereas in the Trojan and Phaestian examples it slopes upwards. The religious signifi-cance of this type of vessel is shown by their appearance in the hands of the mysterious daemons of Mycenaean times.

FIG. 99.—VARIEGATED LIMESTONE (Slightly Enlarged).

Early types of pottery from the Hagios Onuphrios find are represented in Figs. 100, 102, 103. Fig. 100 is of a dark blackish brown colour with per-forated handles for suspension and a cover with four additional handles. The cover is almost identical with one found in the First City of Troy,[9a] and the whole type of vessel, with the perforated, ear-like handles, answers to those of the earliest strata of Hissarlik. Fig. 101, from an early cist-grave at Arvi (see below), is added for the sake of comparison. It too is of the same dark bucchero, but of finer fabric, and it greatly resembles a vase from the earliest settlement at Tiryns.[9b] Fig. 102 is a cover of another

FIG. 100.—PHAESTOS (⅔ diam.).

hanging pot of the same bucchero ware. Fig. 103 is a small spouted vessel of the same dark paste, and Fig. 104 is a small reddish brown

---

[9] In the Central Museum at Athens.

[9a] Schliemann, *Trojanische Alterthümer*, Atlas, Taf. 21, 14 m. *Ilios*, p. 215, No. 27 (upside down).

[9b] Schliemann, *Tiryns*, p. 58, No. 1.

I

vessel with four handles, two of them for suspension with double vertical perforations. The double-horned object of brown bucchero (Fig. 105) strongly recalls the horned handles (*anse cornute*) so characteristic of the

FIG. 101.—ARVI (⅔ diam.).

Italian *terremare*. It is doubtless an attachment of a pot and from the two holes below seems to have been intended to resemble an ox's head. Its nearest parallel is the fragment of a vase representing a horned head of the same kind found in the early cemetery of Agia Paraskevê in Cyprus.

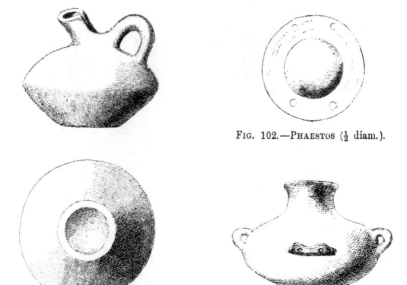

FIG. 102.—PHAESTOS (½ diam.).

FIG. 103.—PHAESTOS (Slightly Reduced).   FIG. 104.—PHAESTOS (Slightly Reduced).

Of a more advanced technique, but still hand-made like the others, are Figs. 106, 107, 108, which show the beginnings of painted ware with a dull surface. The round-bottomed oenochoê (Fig. 105) has a pale yellow ground

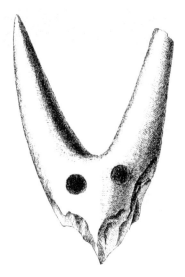

FIG. 105.—TERRACOTTA.   FIG. 106b.—BOTTOM OF SPOUTED VASE.

FIG. 106a —SPOUTED VASE PAINTED PALE YELLOW, WITH TERRACOTTA STRIPES (⅓ Linear).

FIG. 107.—PAINTED PYXIS; White Bands on Terracotta Coloured ground (½ Linear).

COLOURS
R - Red
G - Gray
W - White.

The gray
is a
grayish
black

FIG. 108.—PAINTED VASE (Slightly reduced : 12 cent. high).

with terracotta-coloured stripes. In form and colouring it shows some
affinity to the later class of vases in the Amorgos cemeteries. Fig. 107 is a
kind of pyxis with white bands on a terracotta ground. Originally, no
doubt, it was provided with a cover.

The jar represented in Fig. 108 shows still greater advance in the art of
colouring pottery ; it bears red and white stripes on a greyish black ground,
and its tints agree with those of some of the vessels found in the Kamares
cave, on the Southern side of Mt. Ida.[10]   Indeed, the Kamares pottery must
be brought into very direct relation with Phaestos, within whose territory it
probably lay. On the other hand, the style of colouring shows a distinct
approach to that of the earliest vases from Thera and Therasia. The design
on this jar, and to a certain degree its shape, seems to me to stand in a
direct relation to a very beautiful type of stone vase (Fig. 123) which was
in vogue in prehistoric Crete.

FIG. 109.—PHAESTOS ; LIMESTONE (Natural Size).

Stone vases play a very important part in the early remains of Crete, as
also in the contemporary deposits of Naxos, Amorgos, and other early Aegean
sites. A small limestone vase from the Hagios Onuphrios deposit is given in
Fig. 109, together with its lid of the same material. Except that its cover
is not provided with a knob at top, this vase bears a close resemblance to one
(Fig. 119) obtained by me from a prehistoric cemetery at Arvi, the ancient
Arbi, on the South-Eastern coast of the island. The variegated limestone
vase, Fig. 110, now in the Ashmolean Museum, was found, like Fig. 109,
near Phaestos, and probably belongs to the same early necropolis.

These stone vases form such a characteristic feature in early Cretan
deposits, and seem to afford in certain cases such a definite chronological clue,
that a fuller account of those that I was able to meet with in the course of
my recent explorations may not be amiss. They differ from the stone vessels

---

[10] See above, pp. 79 (348), 81 (350) and note.

of the 'Amorgan Period,' such as are usually found in the prae-Mycenaean deposits of the Aegean islands, in two particulars. The stone-ware such as is discovered for instance in the early tombs of Naxos and Amorgos is generally of white, apparently Parian, marble. The Cretan vessels are of far more varied materials. The other respect in which they differ from the kindred Aegean class is that they show a much greater conformity with certain types of Egyptian [11] and, possibly too, of Libyan stone vessels.[12]

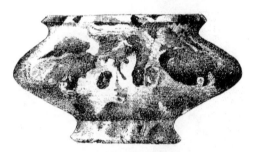

FIG. 110.—PHAESTOS; VARIEGATED LIMESTONE (⅓ diam.).

Massive pots of serpentine and diorite supported by pedestals of limestone or baked clay, forming incense altars, appear in Egyptian tombs from the time of the Fourth Dynasty (Fig. 111), and several of these dating from the Fourth to the Sixth Dynasties are preserved in the Gizeh Museum. They are often provided with perforated horizontal handles, and the rim at top is generally broad and flat.

A dark stone vessel (Fig. 112) found at Pinies above Elunta, the ancient Olous, bears, as will be seen by a comparison with Fig. 111, a very close resemblance to this archaic Egyptian class. A plainer type (Fig. 113) without handles was procured by me at Goulàs, where larger vessels formed of a kind of conglomerate may still be seen beside some of the ancient cisterns Some of these were noticed by Spratt.[13]

Another prolific find-spot of this early Cretan stone-ware is Arvi, the site of the ancient Arbi, on the South-Eastern coast, where there existed an early cemetery of the same period as the sepulchral deposit of Phaestos. Figs. 114, 115, 116, 117, and the clay suspension vase (Fig. 101), were described as having been found here on either side of the head of a skeleton enclosed in a rude stone cist. Figs. 118 and 119 are from the same necropolis. Fig. 118 closely resembles an Egyptian alabaster kohl-pot without its 'collar.' In the case of Figs. 117, 119 both the form of the vessel itself and the knobbed

---

[11] There are however some flat stone vessels from Amorgos, round in outline with four oblong protuberances at the four points of their circumference, which closely resemble a form of Egyptian stone 'patera,' often provided with a spout.

[12] Mr. Petrie writes to me from Nagada on the Upper Nile that he believes to have located near there the manufacture of many of the finer forms of stone vessels found in Egypt in a settlement of an unknown race, possibly Libyan, the date of which he places between the Sixth and Eleventh Dynasties. Like the Cretan, these vessels have flat bases.

[13] *Travels in Crete*, vol. i. p. 135.

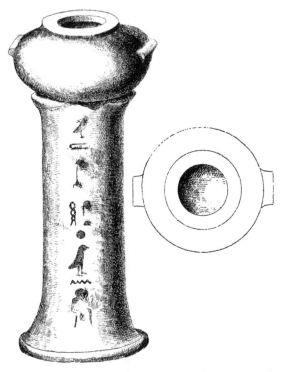

FIG. 111.—EGYPTIAN INCENSE VASE OF SERPENTINE ON LIMESTONE.   FOURTH DYNASTY.

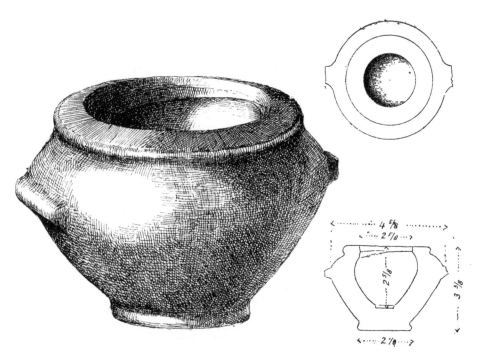

FIG. 112.—BROWN STONE VASE, PINIES, ELUNTA (OLOUS).   ⅓ diam.

lids that surmount them are almost identical with that or stone vases found
in Twelfth Dynasty deposits. A steatite lid of this date from Kahun [14] (Fig.
120) might have been made for the same pot as Fig. 115. It thus appears
that the early stone vessels of Crete bear witness like the seals [15] to an
intimate contact with the Nile Valley as early as the first half of the Third
millennium before our era. In view of such early parallels as are suggested
by Fig. 112 we may indeed well ask ourselves whether this Egyptian influence
may not date back to a time anterior even to the Twelfth Dynasty. It is
true that the flattening of the bottom distinguishes these Cretan types
from the very earliest class of Egyptian stone vessels, which are rounded
below, and that the hieroglyph for 'granite' is in fact a round-bottomed
vessel of this class. Vessels of basalt, alabaster, and other materials, with
a flat base and otherwise greatly resembling some of the Cretan types, were
however already known under the Early Empire.[15b] They were common, as
we now know from Mr. Petrie's recent researches, among the Libyans of the
Upper Nile before the time of the Eleventh Dynasty.

The flat steatite bowl (Fig. 121) is interesting from its having been found
in the cave sanctuary of Psychro on Mount Lasethe, probably the *Diktaion
Antron* of the Lyttians.[16] Fig. 122 from Chersonêsos is specially remarkable
from the beauty of its material, a limestone conglomerate, and from the
evident traces of some kind of turning.

Of all the forms of early stone vases found in Crete the most artistic is
certainly that reproduced in Fig. 123, which has already been referred to as
affording a probable suggestion for the decoration of the painted jar from
Phaestos (Fig. 108). Massive as it is, the graceful foliations that surround it
give it almost the appearance of a flower-cup embedded in its calix. That
this elegant type of vessel was once much in vogue in the island is indicated
by the fact that I came across two similar examples, one on the Northern, the
other on the Southern coast of Crete. The latter was from a site known to
the natives from the ancient pots found there as 'Pharmakokephali,' which
perhaps may be translated 'Gallipot Head,' on or near the site of the ancient
Ampelos.[16b] The other (Fig. 123) was obtained by me at Mílato, the ancient
Miletos, and was said to have been found within two feet of a curious pot
of a shape suggestive of a 'swallow's-nest' [17] in what seems to have been an
ancient grave. Both the elegant contour of this type of stone vessel and the
apparent influence of the design on the earliest painted pottery of the island,
approaching in date that of Santorin and Therasia, seem to bring these vases
down to the latest prae-Mycenaean period. Stone vessels continued, as is well

---

[14] Given me by Professor Petrie.

[15] See above, p. 57 (326) *seqq.*

[15b] In the recent Exhibition of Egyptian
Antiquities at the Burlington Club, London,
was an alabaster vase of the Early Empire, with
a flat base, greatly resembling that from Pinies
(Fig. 112), and another bowl of black basalt of
the same early period, somewhat resembling

below the steatite bowl from Psychro (Fig. 121).

[16] See *Academy*, June 1, 1895, p. 469.

[16b] This specimen was given by me to the
Museum of the Syllogos at Candia.

[17] Two other vessels of this form procured by
Professor Halbherr in the Province of Siteia are
now in the Museum of the Syllogos at Candia.

FIG. 113.—GOULÀS; GREY STEATITE (⅔ diam.).

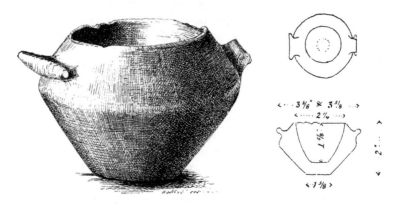

FIG. 114.—CIST GRAVE, ARVI; STEATITE (⅔ diam.).

FIG. 115.—CIST GRAVE, ARVI;
STEATITE (⅔ diam.).

FIG. 116.—CIST GRAVE, ARVI;
STEATITE (⅔ diam.).

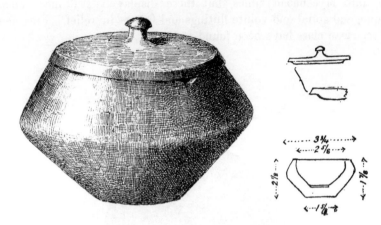

FIG. 117.—CIST GRAVE, ARVI; STEATITE (⅔ diam.).

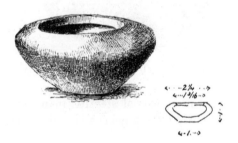

FIG. 118.—ARVI; LIMESTONE (⅔ diam.).

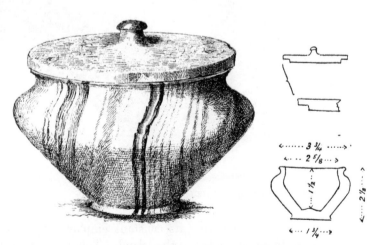

FIG. 119.—ARVI; BANDED LIMESTONE (⅔ diam.).

known, into Mycenaean times, but these display a still more advanced technique, and spiral and volute flutings and figures in relief. Fragments of this Mycenaean class have been found at Knôsos.

FIG. 120.—STEATITE LID, TWELFTH DYNASTY DEPOSIT, KAHUN, EGYPT (⅔ diam.).

The vases are for the most part of steatite, in many cases approaching that made use of for the early Cretan gems and seal-stones. Where this was

FIG. 121.—CAVE, PSYCHRO; STEATITE (⅔ diam.).

procured is as yet a mystery, but from its constant employment it seems probable that it exists in great masses in the island. The material of Fig.

112 is less easily definable; its harder texture and the porphyritic crystals that it contains are both noteworthy. The banded limestone of **Fig. 119** seems to be foreign to Crete.

FIG. 122.—CHERSONÊSOS; LIMESTONE CONGLOMERATE (⅔ diam.).

It is evident with regard to the technique that in most cases the vases have been turned, and it looks as if in Crete the use of the wheel for stone vases may have preceded its application to clay. It is a significant fact that the clay vessels found with the stone pots (Figs. 114, 115, 116,

FIG. 123.—MÍLATO; STEATITE (⅔ diam.).

117) from Arvi and that from Mílato were hand-made, though in the former case at any rate the stone vases from the same grave had the appearance of having been turned. The stone vases were further finished by scraping or chiselling.

I am indebted to Mr. J. L. Myres for the following detailed notes on the material and fabric of the above stone vases.

Fig. 112. Black matrix, with dull brown patches, which appear to be slightly softer, and numerous well-defined long porphyritic crystals of yellowish white colour. Harder than the other vases but scratched without difficulty with the knife, and slightly absorbent to the touch in spite of the comparatively high polish. (Pinies, Elunta.)

Fig. 113. Steatite, greyish white with indistinct lighter and softer streaks. Split by heat on one side. Partly turned, partly scraped. (Goulàs.)

Fig 114. Steatite; blackish brown, with wavy structure and white patches which are softer; turned on the lathe. (Arvi.)

Fig. 115. Steatite; greyish with indistinct light coloured patches rather harder but less dense than Figs. 114, 116. The lid with this is of steatite; black compact ground with distinct white patches which are softer. It is partly turned, partly scraped or ground. (Arvi.)

Fig. 116. Steatite; black with irregular white patches which are softer. Turned on the lathe and finished outside with a knife or a chisel. (Arvi.)

Fig. 117. Steatite; black compact ground with rather rarer white patches. Partly turned, partly rubbed. (Arvi.)

Figs. 114–117 seem to be of the same origin, though their qualities vary slightly. [They are from the same group of early tombs at Arvi.]

Fig. 118. Limestone; compact, greyish; mottled with white calcspar; not unlike specimens of common cretaceous limestone of the Levant. Turned. (Arvi.)

Fig. 119. Limestone; compact and slightly argillaceous, finely banded in grey and cream white. (Arvi.)

This material is not known in Crete, nor likely to occur there. The steatite lid with this did not originally belong to it. Its material much resembles that of Fig. 113. It is partly turned, partly rubbed.

Fig. 120. Steatite; blackish brown with reddish patches which are softer but less 'weathered' than Figs. 114–117. Partly turned, partly rubbed, and with a good surface polish. (From Kahun, Egypt.)

Fig. 121. Steatite; compact, brownish and very soft, much damaged. (Psychro Cave.)

Fig. 122. Limestone breccia; white, pink and yellow, red matrix. Not known in Crete. (Chersonesos.)

Fig. 123. Steatite; greyish, with indistinct lighter and softer patches and streaks; very like Fig. 113. No traces of turning; cut and scraped. (Milato.)

Figs. 113 and 121 and the lid of Fig. 118 very closely resemble one another, and might very well be from the same mass.

Among the stone objects discovered at Hagios Onuphrios the marble 'idols,' of which sketches are given below in Figs. 124—132 [18], are of essentially the same class as those found in Amorgos and other Greek islands. The series here brought to light bears witness to a degree of evolution of form which seems to indicate the lapse of a considerable period of time. Figs. 124—126 may be compared with the simplest Trojan examples. In Fig. 131, on the other hand, we have a more advanced type, in which the arms are clearly drawn laid across the body just below the breasts, and the breasts themselves are in full relief. In Figs. 127—130 we have various intermediate types. Fig. 134 is a head alone with two perforations in the neck for attachment.

To these Phaestian specimens I am able to add two other Cretan examples said to have been found in the Province of Siteia (Figs. 133, 134).

---

[18] The small image represented in Fig. 127 is now in the Ashmolean Museum. It was acquired by me at Candia and was stated by its possessor to have been found at Phaestos. It probably belongs to the same deposit, and in any case illustrates the same period of local culture.

FIG. 124 (Slightly Enlarged).

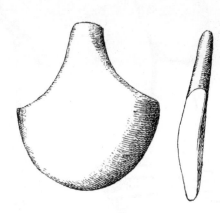

FIG. 126 (Natural Size).

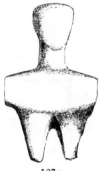

127a

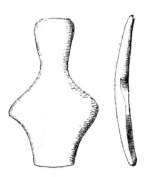

FIG. 125 (Natural Size).

127b

FIG. 127
(Natural Size).

FIG. 128 (Natural Size).

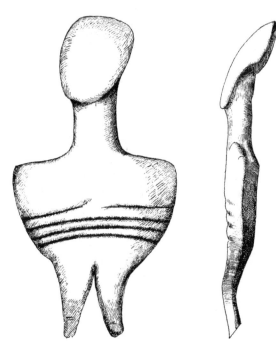

FIG. 132 (Slightly Enlarged).

FIG. 129 (Natural Size).

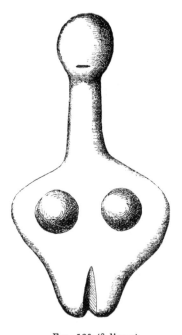

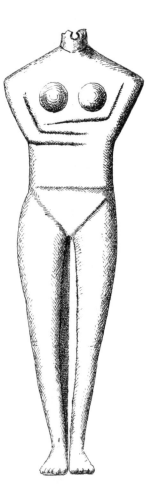

FIG. 130 (⅔ linear).

FIG. 131 (⅔ linear).

Like the others, they are of Parian marble, so that the material at least must have been imported.

An exhaustive discussion of the various questions raised by these curious figures would require a separate dissertation. Here it must be sufficient to remark that the theory according to which we have simply to deal with degenerate copies from Chaldaean prototypes representing Istar or the Mother Goddess does not accord with the evidence at present before us.

The simpler forms of these Aegean figures are so lacking in detail as to afford no definite points of comparison with the Asiatic types in question. On the other hand, if we turn to the West and North, we find a whole series of early images of clay, stone, and other materials which certainly seem to fit on to these Aegean forms. From the remains of the early settlements of Troy, we know that simple forms of this class of figures occur indifferently in marble, clay, and bone. Alabaster and clay figures of the same class are scattered through the Thracian lands and beyond the Danube as far afield as Roumania [19] and the valley of the Maros in Transylvania. But beyond the Carpathians again there appears another parallel class of primitive figures which must perhaps be regarded as the most characteristic product of a vast Neolithic Province including a large part of Poland, East Prussia, and Western Russia. Stalagmite figures of this kind have been found in the Polish Caves,[20] on the East-Prussian coast they recur in amber,[21] and a bone figure of the same kind has been found by Inostranzeff in the remains of a Neolithic station on the shore of Lake Ladoga.[22] These Northern figures do not exhibit indeed any marked indications of sex. On one amber example, however, the body is marked by an imperfect triangular outline which resembles the representation of the vulva on some of the Trojan or Aegean types. The double perforation at the junction of the neck and body which characterizes some of the Baltic and Russian examples recalls the perforations on the neck of the 'idols' from Phaestos and Siteia represented in Figs. 133, 134, and that of the head by itself in Fig. 132.[23] The holes and grooves on some of the Baltic forms suggest attachment to other objects, and a marble figure from an Amorgan cist (Fig. 135) shows lines upon it which seem to indicate the same application.[23b] It would be unwise to insist too much on these resemblances in detail, but taken in connexion with the appearance of this parallel class of Northern figures they can hardly be without some significance.

---

[19] Primitive clay statuettes have been found at Cucuteni in Roumania (*Antiqua*, 1890, Taf. v. 2). Cf. *Bulletin de la Société d'Anthropologie*, 1889, p. 582, and S. Reinach, *Anthropologie*, 1894, p. 293.

[20] Ossowski iv. Zbiór Wiadomosci do Antropologii Krajowej. (Third report on Polish Caves, *op. cit.* (1881) I. vi. pp. 28–51, Pl. iii.–v.) Matériaux, 1882, pp. 1-24, Pl. I. II. Tischler, *Steinzeit in Ostpreussen*, pp. 96, 97.

[21] Tischler, *Steinzeit in Ostpreussen*, p. 25 (g), Figs. 6, 7 (*Schriften d. phys.-oek. Ges.*, Königs-berg, 1882).

[22] Tischler, *op. cit.* 118 (30) Fig. 10.

[23] On a marble idol from Amorgos (Ashmolean Coll.) the thighs are bored.

[23b] Now in the Ashmolean Museum. This figure shows signs of painting on the right side of the neck, apparently representing a pendant lock of hair. This is the same figure as that sketched by Dr. Wolters (*Ath. Mitth.* 1891 p. 49 Fig. 3) and is from Grave D described by Dr. Dümmler (*Ath. Mitth.* 1886, p. 15 *seqq.*).

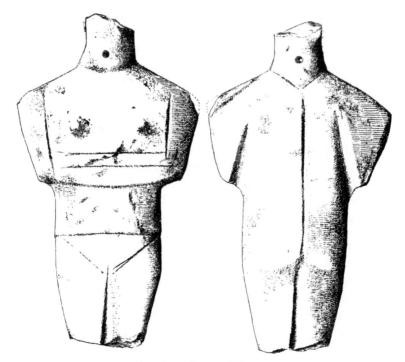

FIG. 133.—SITEIA (⅔ linear).

FIG. 134.—SITEIA (⅜ linear).

K

The Aegean and Northern group together occupy in fact a continuous zone roughly divided by the Carpathians. It would even appear that this zone had a Libyan extension. A clay female figure acquired by Mr. Petrie [24] from Abusir, near Sameineh, in the middle of the Delta, must clearly be regarded as a somewhat developed offshoot from the same primitive family. The lower part of this 'idol' resembles the Greek island figures, but the side-lock on the head gives this foreign relic from Egyptian soil a typically Libyan aspect. Small images in a squatting posture were also found by Mr. Petrie in his recently discovered settlement of an unknown, probably

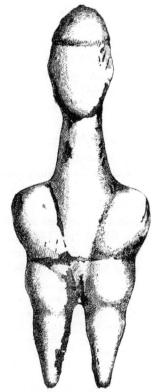

FIG. 135.—CIST GRAVE, AMORGOS (Natural Size).

Libyan, race on the Upper Nile. These recall a class of squatting, obese female figures that may be traced from Thrace to Attica and the Peloponnese and which in turn curiously resemble the so called 'Cabiri' found in the prehistoric building known as Hagiar Kím in Malta,[24b]—a structure the

[24] See *Illahun, Kahun and Gurob*, Pl. xix. 43, and p. 19. It might also be an interesting question how far the Egyptian wooden dolls ending above in a rectangular stump, to which the beadstrings are tied to represent hair, may go back to primitive types of 'idols' resembling the Aegean. The parallelism is sometimes striking.

[24b] Caruana *Report on the Phoenician &c. Antiquities of Malta*, pp. 30, 31 and photograph: Furse, *Prehistoric Congress, Norwich*, p. 412 and Pl. ii. Perrot et Chipiez, T. iii. *Phénicie*, &c., p. 305, Figs. 230, 231, where the Hagiar Kím itself, this counterpart of Talyots and chambered barrows, reappears as a 'Phoenician Temple.'

affinities of which point in almost equal degrees to North Africa and the Iberian West.

Proceeding westwards we find the X-like lines on the bodies of some Trojan figures [25] recurring in a more decorative form on the female clay 'idol' from the Laibach pile-settlement, and on another primitive image from the prehistoric Station at Butmir in Bosnia.[25b] Not to speak of some general resemblances presented by certain rude clay images found in the Swiss Lake dwellings and Italian *terremare*, recent discoveries on the Tyrrhene and still more westerly Mediterranean shores have supplied parallels of a very interesting kind. In the Finale Caves on the old Ligurian coast have been found clay figures [26] of 'Aeneolithic' date approaching those of Hissarlik and perhaps affording the nearest prototypes to Mycenaean forms. In Spain again the Brothers Siret have found figures of schist and bone in Neolithic and early Bronze Age deposits [27] which seem to stand in a direct relationship to the Aegean 'idols.' A whale-bone figure was found with Neolithic relics at Skara in Orkney, and images with the attributes of maternity strongly emphasized were already known to the European population of the Reindeer Period.[27b]

In view of these widely ramifying and deeply-rooted European connexions [27c] it seems in the highest degree unsafe to assume that the earliest Aegean 'idols' of the present class are nothing more than degenerate copies of early Chaldaean images. Rather it is reasonable to suppose that the widespread primitive custom may have had a more easterly extension as far as the valley of the Euphrates. From the frequent association of these images with interments alike in the Aegean islands, the Ligurian caves, and South-Eastern Spain, we are led to infer that they had some connexion with ideas relating to the Nether World. This view is in fact supported by parallels from remote

---

[25] *E.g.* Schliemann, *Troy*, p. 331, Fig. 193.

[25b] Radimsky und Hoernes, *Die Neolithische Station von Butmir bei Sarajevo in Bosnien*, Taf. ii. 2.

[26] See A. Issel, *Liguria Geologica e Prehistorica* Tav. xxviii. Figs. 11 and 14, and my 'Prehistoric Interments of the Balzi-Rossi Caves and their relation to the Cave-Burials of the Finalese' (*Anthr. Inst. Journ.*, 1893 p. 306 and note), where attention is called to the fact that one of these primitive images is painted and belongs to the Ligurian class of Neolithic painted pottery. (Cf. G. B. Amerano, *Dei Vasi colorati e dipinti delle Caverne di Finale*.) These vases are the Ligurian counterparts of the prae-Mycenaean class of Sikel (or Sikan) painted ware. A somewhat more advanced painted figure was found in a neolithic 'cave' tomb, Villafrati near Palermo.

[27] *Premiers Ages de Métal dans le Sud-Est de l'Espagne*, pp. 32, 57, 257, and Plates vi. and ix. ; *La fin de l'epoque neolithique en Espagne*, in *Anthropologie*, 1892, pp. 387, 399.

[27b] For the 'Venus of Brassempouy,' and other ivory figurines from the same sub-Pyrenaean grotto, see *Anthropologie*, T. vi. (1895), p. 141 *sqq.*

[27c] Since this was written I have had an opportunity of perusing M. Salomon Reinach's articles entitled 'La Sculpture en Europe avant les influences gréco-romaines' (*Anthropologie*, 1894, 15–34, 173–186, 288–305 ; 1895, 18–39, 293–311). In these M. Reinach, like myself, lays stress on the parallelism presented by the Trojan and Aegean forms of primitive images with those of Spain, the Danubian regions, and the Amber Coast of the Baltic. He also maintains that these European forms were evolved from the rudest and simplest prototypes rather than that they degenerated from higher models : 'Étant donné un pilier ou une tablette quadrangulaire, on pouvait d'abord, pour suggérer l'idée de la forme humaine, amincir certaines parties, telle que la taille et le cou, de manière à faire saillir les épaules et la tête' (*op. cit.* 1894, p. 291).

parts of the globe. In Japan there is actually a historic record of the substitution in place of the slaves and retainers who sacrificed themselves to
their deceased lord of small figures deposited in his grave. The Ushabtis or
'Répondants' of the Egyptian tombs are said to have had a similar object,
and it was their function to act as substitutes for the dead person when his
turn came to work in the fields below. In ancient Mexican graves terracotta
heads are of frequent occurrence, which seem to have been attached to figures
of more perishable material[28] and to have represented the wives or slaves of
the departed. It is probable that the Phaestos head with two holes in the
neck was also made for attachment to a body of some less lasting substance.

What we have to deal with then is an 'Aegean' version of a primitive
funereal custom which both in the Western Mediterranean basin and in the
Danubian and Baltic lands seems to have had a wide European extension over
a continuous area. In the Egyptian Ushabtis we have perhaps a conventionalized type of what may have originally been a southern offshoot of one
archaic family. The occurrence of clay 'idols' of the same general character
in Cypriote 'Copper Age' cemeteries like that of Alambra shows an Asiatic
extension of the same custom, and we are thus led to the curious nude
figures seen on early Chaldaean cylinders.[29]

These nude images have in this case been plausibly connected with the
legend of the Goddess Istar, who, in order to pass through the seven gates of
'the Unchanging Land without return'—there to procure the Waters of Life
for her 'wounded Thammuz'—was forced to strip herself one by one of her
robes and jewels till she went in at last mother-naked. It is certain that a
direct piece of evidence connects them with her double—the Goddess Sala.
Although no similar Chaldaean images of clay and stone are known of
this early date, the absolute correspondence in type presented by
Asiatic clay figures of a much later period permits us to suppose that more
archaic examples will some day be brought to light. The connexion
with the visit of the Mother Goddess to the abode of Death is just such a
mythic outgrowth from the primitive custom of burying the naked image of a
wife or mother with the departed as might have been expected. It was also
inevitable—admitting such a mythic superstructure—that the Eastern family
of such funereal images should afterwards undergo a religious transformation
and be identified with or assimilated to Istar or some one or other of her
Asiatic equivalents. The Syrian influence, resulting in a more sensuous
type of female image, with the organs of maternity strongly emphasized,
undoubtedly spread through Anatolia, and early left its mark on the clay
figures of the Cypriote graves. It may however be laid down as an absolute
rule that the earlier the image the less trace there is of any such Asiatic

---

[28] E. B. Tylor, *Anahuac*, p. 229.

[29] See, for examples, Menant, *Glyptique
Orientale* i. p. 172, pp. 173-175 ; Figs. 110-116.
Menant regarded the connexion with Istar as in
these cases 'not proven,' Nikolsky, however
(*Rev. Arch.* 1891, ii. p. 41), has now shown that
on one cylinder this and a nude male figure that
often occurs with it are identified by the inscription with Sala and Ramanu, in many respects
reduplicate forms of Istar and Tammuz.
Ramanu is the Syrian Rimmon,

PRIMITIVE CRETAN AND AEGEAN CULTURE. 132

influence. The figures in the earliest deposits of Hissarlik—those of the
First City—are absolutely primitive and the most removed from all suggestion
of these supposed Chaldaean prototypes. The existence of a continuous group
of primitive 'idols' on European soil going back to Neolithic times, and
extending from Crete to the shores of Lake Ladoga in one direction and to
the Pillars of Hercules in the other, must in the absence of very direct
evidence to the contrary be regarded as an independent phenomenon.

So far as existing evidence goes, at the time when the Istar model first
reached the Aegean shores their inhabitants were already in the age of
metals, and it appears as an intrusive form beside the more primitive idols
which they had handed down from Neolithic times. A leaden female image
found by Dr. Schliemann in the second city of Hissarlik [30] clearly betrays its
oriental parentage. The swastika engraved on the vulva is also evidently a
stamp of godhead. This figure in turn finds its parallel in one of a pair of male
and female divinities that appear on a serpentine mould, now in the Louvre,
found at Selendj, East of Thyatira in the ancient Maeonia [31] (Fig. 135),
and these figures, as M. Salomon Reinach has shown,[32] take us back again
to another Asiatic mould of the same material in which a God and Goddess
are once more represented side by side. In this latter example the God
with the horned headpiece evidently stands for a form of Bel, while his
female companion, though in this case her lower limbs are draped after the
flounced Babylonian fashion,[33] bears on her head a curious rayed half circle,
which sufficiently betrays her identity. It is, in fact, the upper part of that
special variety of the radiate disk which in Chaldean symbolism indicates
the star of Istar.

The Western influence of the Babylonian type would find a curious
illustration if we might accept the genuineness of a lead figure said to have
been found with another lead object exhibiting cruciform ornaments near
Candia. These objects were obtained in 1889 by Mr. Greville Chester, and
are now in the Ashmolean Collection (Fig. 136). But both the figure and
the ornaments are almost line for line identical with the female divinity and
two of the engraved objects that appear on the Selendj mould. It almost
looks as if they had been actually cast in this individual mould, and if their
claim to antiquity is to be allowed it would result that these leaden objects
were imported into Crete from Maeonia in prehistoric times. The figure has
the appearance of great age, but it is possible that some Levantine dealer
may have profited by the existence of the mould to cast some lead figures
from it. The fact that the square ornament is broken off at the same point

[30] *Ilios*, p. 337, Fig. 226. The Babylonian
parentage of this figure was clearly pointed out
by Sayce in his Preface to Schliemann's *Troja*,
pp. xviii., xix. He identifies the image with
the Trojan Atè and 'Athi, the Great Goddess of
Carchemish. He thus traces the type to
Chaldaea through Hittite mediation.

[31] S. Reinach, *Esquisses Archéologiques* (1888),
p. 45 (by whose kind permission it is here re-

produced), and cf. Perrot et Chipiez v. p. 300
Fig. 209.
[32] *Op. cit.* p. 46.
[33] The draped lower limbs bring us nearer to
Mycenaean types. Compare especially the im-
pressed glass figures of a female divinity from
Tomb II. of the lower city, Mycenae. Tsountas,
Ἀνασκαφαὶ τάφων ἐν Μυκήναις, Ἐφ. Ἀρχ. 1888,
Pl. viii. 9.

as that on the mould as it at present exists is certainly suspicious, and the lead itself had been simply poured liquid on to one face of the mould instead of being introduced by a duct between the two halves of which the mould originally consisted. The back of the figure and ornaments has thus no moulding at all. It seems then that we have to deal with leaden casts taken in modern times from a mould probably identical with that in the Louvre.

The Babylonian characteristics of the Selendj type are even more clearly marked than in the Trojan example. The curls beside the head, the arms a-kimbo meeting under the breasts, and the curiously angular thighs recall the salient features already referred to, as seen on the Chaldaean cylinders.

FIG. 136.—SERPENTINE MOULD, SELENDJ.

The mere fact however that the Hissarlik image is of lead shows that at the time when it was made the inhabitants of the Western part of Anatolia to which it belongs were already in the metallurgic stage of culture. Nor do the objects, probably amulets relating to the cult of the deities whose images they here surround on the mould, seem to indicate the most primitive period. The find-spot of the Hissarlik figure in the 'Burnt City,' at a depth of twenty-three feet, points nevertheless to a very early date, and the Phaestos deposit supplies a piece of evidence which fits in with this, the occurrence namely of two perforated seals (Figs. 86, 87), one of grey steatite, the other of ivory, which reproduce both the round and the square cruciform ornaments of the Selendj mould.

It thus appears that during the period covered by the remains of the Second City of Troy, to which in part at least the Phaestos deposit can be shown on other evidence to go back,[34] Chaldaean influences were making themselves felt on the Aegean shores, a fact also attested by the early occurence both at Troy and in contemporary island deposits of native imitations of Babylonian cylinders.

The possibility of Chaldaean influence on the more advanced of the marble figures from the Phaestos deposit, as of those from the contemporary

FIG. 137.—LEAD FIGURES SAID TO BE FROM CANDIA.   (Nat. Size.)

cist-graves of Amorgos, cannot therefore be altogether excluded, and the question resolves itself simply into one of degree. If the parallels cited above lead us to infer the existence of a primitive class of indigenous figures throughout a wide European area which may indeed have been the common property of old Chaldaea, we have on the other hand evidence of a return

[34] See above, p. 57 (326) *seqq.*

wave from the East due to the influence of Babylonian and Asiatic cults
which recast in a new mould the later Aegean forms.[34b]

As a matter of fact there are certain features on the more advanced forms
of the Aegean marble 'idols' which may with some probability be ascribed to this
influence.

1. In the leaden image from Troy as well as on the figure of Istar on the
Maeonian mould necklaces are indicated round the neck. These are traceable
on some Trojan and Amorgan figures and apparently on Fig. 131 from Phaestos.

2. The angular widening of the thighs, specially noticeable in an example
from Delphi,[35] has an Asiatic look.

3. On a marble figure from a cist-grave at Amorgos (Fig. 135), already
noticed as apparently showing signs of binding, there seems to be traceable on
one side of the head a curling lock of hair painted on the stone, which recalls
the sidelocks of the lead figures.

4. The male type which is occasionally found among the more developed
specimens has, in the case of one example from Amorgos,[36] a conical headpiece divided into tiers or zones which recalls that of the male god, probably
a form of Bel, associated with Istar on the Asiatic mould in the Cabinet des

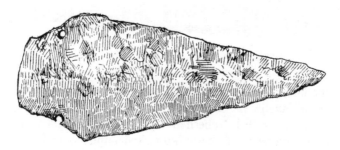

FIG. 138.—BRONZE DAGGER, PHAESTOS.   (⅔ Linear).

Médailles.[37] Traces of a conical cap are visible on the Amorgan idol (Fig. 137).

It remains for us to consider the bronze weapons from the Phaestos
deposit, of which however only two specimens are preserved.

The flat bronze dagger-blade (Fig. 138) is of a form which also occurs in
the early cist-graves of Amorgos. The other bronze weapon given in Fig. 139
is of a more original and hitherto unique character, and must be regarded as a
double-pointed spear-head. It will be remembered that in a far more
developed stage the double-pointed spear or javelin occurs as a characteristic
weapon in the hands of a Lycaonian warrior on the well-known stele of
Iconium.[38] It looks then as if the H. Onuphrios deposit presents us with the

---

[34b] I am wholly unable to follow M. Reinach
in his attempt (*Rev. Arch.* 1895, p. 367 *seqq.*
*Les déesses nues dans l'art oriental et dans l'art
grec*) to trace the Oriental nude figures—and
even those on the Chaldaean cylinders—to
' Aegean ' influences.

[35] *Athen. Mittheilungen*, 1881, p. 361.
[36] In the Polytechnion at Athens.
[37] S. Reinach, *Esquisses Archéologiques*, p. 46.
[38] Texier, *Description de l'Asie Mineure* ii.
148, 149, and Pl. ciii. ; Perrot et Chipiez, T. iv.
p. 741, Fig. 359.

prototype of a class of weapon which had a long-continued existence on the Asianic side. The Lycaonian form indeed suggests a further connexion with the curious two-pronged implements of bronze of which so many examples have been found at Tel Nebesheh. These were derived from tombs apparently belonging to mercenaries brought over by Psamtik I. when he settled Carians and Ionians at Defenneh.[39] Professor Petrie describes the tombs in question as 'Cypriote' but no bronze objects of the kind seem to be known in Cyprus. From the fact that they often occur in association with spear-heads, and from the cross piece that in some cases appears between the prongs, Mr. Petrie inclined to believe that they were the butt-ends of spears,

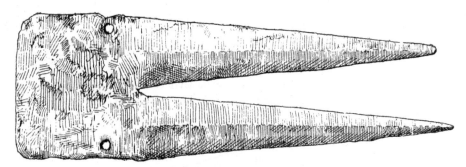

FIG. 139.—DOUBLE-POINTED BRONZE SPEAR, PHAESTOS.   (⅔ Linear).

forked like the lower ends of Egyptian sceptres. The existence of a double-pointed spear or javelin in Crete and Lycaonia, coupled with the Carian connexion in which the Tel Nebesheh objects stand, makes it just possible however that the presence of these two-forked implements in the graves of these mercenaries may be due to some religious survival keeping up the form of an old national weapon for funereal usage.

---

[39] W. M. Flinders Petrie, *Tanis*, Pt. II. Pl. iii. and pp. 20, 21. The tombs date from the Eighth to the Fifth Century, B.C.

SUPPLEMENTARY NOTES.

The following supplementary notes are mainly the result of a visit to Crete, in company with Mr. J. L. Myres, during the spring of this year.

In the neighbourhood of Retimo (Rhithymna) I heard of the existence of a 'Column' on which was a sign ⊞ resembling No. 26 on Table I. (p. 349) which is seen on a block of the prehistoric building at Knôsos (see p. 282, Fig. 9*f*) and again on the amphora handle from Mycenae (see p. 273, Fig. 2). In this case however the central prong is of the same length as the others being continued across the square part of the symbol, and in this respect it is identical with a variety of what is evidently the same sign found at Kahun. Owing to the jealousy of the owner of the land and the belief in buried treasure I was not at the time able to investigate further the remains with which this sign was here associated. I may add that the recent excavations executed on behalf of the British Museum at Curium in Cyprus have resulted in the discovery of two more linear signs of Mycenaean pottery. One of these resembles No. 18 of Table I. The other is an upright with a central prong on one side. Fresh discoveries of signs on Cretan seal-stones have been made by Professor Halbherr, Dr. Mariani, and Dr. Taramelli.

The four-sided seal-stone, Fig. 32, p. 25 (294), now in the Ashmolean Museum at Oxford was labelled by its original possessor, Mr. Greville Chester, as having been found at Sparta. I saw however an impression of the same gem in the hands of a private proprietor at Candia who had formerly possessed it and learnt from him that it was obtained in Crete, though he was unable to inform me of its exact find-spot. Judging from its material, a red cornelian, it probably came from the easternmost part of the island.

In the same hands at Candia I saw the impression of a three-sided seal-stone, on one side of which were grouped the pictographs, Nos. 5 (bent leg) and 25 (gate) while on the two other faces respectively were a wolf and an insect, perhaps a spider.

Another three-sided cornelian seal-stone procured by me from Messarà, bearing on its respective sides a stag, a dog or wolf, and a bird, bore the impress of a somewhat later art, and seems to show that this form of gem may have survived in parts of the island to the verge of the classical period. The stag's antlers were of a curiously conventional form, closely agreeing with that represented on one of the bronze pateras from the cave of the Idaean Zeus.[40] This points to a date approaching 700 B.C.

The three-sided stone from Smyrna (Fig. 53, p. 334) probably also belongs to somewhat later date than most of the Cretan seal-stones of the trilateral type. The cap or helmet on the man's head on the second side

---

[40] *Antichità dell' Antro di Zeus Ideo*, F. Halbherr e P. Orsi. Atlas, Pl. VIII.

represented occurs on a class of seal represented by specimens from Sidon and elsewhere belonging to a period contemporary with that of the geometrical style in Greece.

Similar comparisons lead me to believe that some at least of the flat discoid types of Cretan seal-stones represented in Figs. 66, p. 342, and 67, p. 343, also belong to this later period. The archer on Fig. 66, with his bird-like head, certainly suggests reminiscences of the 'Dipylon' style and its congeners of about the ninth century B.C. A green steatite gem of the same form as the above, acquired by me in Greece, exhibits moreover a figure of a spearman with something like the 'Dipylon' crest, and it is further to be observed that on some seals from the Heraeon at Argos, apparently belonging to the geometrical period, are seen figures of men in tunics bearing a family likeness to those on these two Cretan stones.

I have to thank M. J. P. Six, of Amsterdam, for suggestions of various comparisons between the pictographs and linear signs of Crete and Lykian, Carian and other characters. The Lykian comparisons are especially important from the tradition recorded by Herodotos [41] and corroborated by place-names that the Lykians originally came from Crete. In the neighbouring Pisidia was a Κρητῶν πόλις : in Lykia itself the town-names Aptera and Einatos are common to Crete and on the Lykian borders was both a town and mountain called Daedala.

---

[41] *Hist.* lib. i. 173. Cf. Hoeck, *Creta* ii. p. 335 *seqq.*

INDEX

INDEX.

Mycenaean affinities of Cretan pictographs, [317], 48 *seqq.*
  ceiling design restored from template symbol and gem, [322], 53.
  art in Crete, closely allied with that of Peloponnese, [361], 92.
  distinct from Hittite, [370], 101.
  gems of Crete compared with Peloponnesian, [360], 91.
  gold ring, with cult scene, [361], 92.
Myres, Mr. J. L., his account of the Kamares pottery, [350 *n.*], 81.
  on the Cretan stone vases, 124.

Naue, Dr. Julius, on sp.ral ornament, [329 *n.*], 60, [330 *n.*], 61.
Nagada, early settlement at, 117 *n.*
Nikolsky, on nude figures of Chaldaean cylinders, 131 *n.*

Oaxos (Axos), form of *Vau* at, [360], 91.
Orchomenos, Mycenaean ceiling of, [322], 53.
Orsi, Prof. Paolo, on cave of Idaean Zeus, [354], 85.
  on Cretan ossuary, [319 *n.*], 50.
Ostrich, apparent representation of, on early seal-stone, [341], 72.
Ox, pictograph, [309], 40.
Ox's head, pictograph, [309], 40.

Paladru, Isère, linear signs on pottery of pile-dwellings at, [352 *n.*], 83.
Palaekastro, perhaps Grammion, near Itanos, [276], 7.
  pictographic seal from, [297], 28.
Perrot, M., denies existence of Mycenaean script, [274], 5.
Petrie, Prof. W. M. Flinders, excavations at Koptos, [318], 49.
  on Maket Tomb, Kahun, [318], 49.
  on 'cowroids,' [326 and *n.*], 57.
  on spiral ornament of Egyptian scarab, [330 *n.*], 61.
  on 'Aegean' signs on potsherds of Kahun and Gurob, [348], 79.
  on date of Kahun rubbish-heaps, [348–351], 79–82.
  his discovery of early settlement at Nagada, 117 *n.*, 119, 129.
Phaestos, block with linear signs discovered at, by Prof. Halbherr, [283], 14.
  engraved whorl from deposit at Hagios Onuphrios near, [284], 15.
  seal-stones from do., [284], 15, [285], 16, [325], 56.
  (See Hagios Onuphrios.)
Pharmakokephali, stone vases from, 119.
Philistines, connected with Kefti, [369], 100 *seqq.*

Philistines—continued.
  representatives of Mycenaean culture, [368], 99 *seqq.*
  important part played by, in East Mediterranean basin, [368], 99 *seqq.*
  of Askalon oppress Sidon, [368], 99.
  Palestine, landmark of their conquests, [368], 99.
  commercial instinct of, perceptible in seizure of Gaza, [368], 99.
  Cherethites or Cretans important members of their confederation, [368], 99, [369], 100.
  probably identical with 'Pulasati,' [369 and *n.*], 100.
  Ἕλληνες in LXX. version of Isaiah, [369], 100.
  their city Dore or Dor perhaps Dorian settlement, [369], 100.
  brought by Hebrew tradition from Isle of Caphtor, [369], 100.
  probably from Crete and Aegean Isles, [369], 100 *seqq.*
Phoenician alphabet, comparison of letters of, with Cretan signs, pictographic and linear, [364], 95 *seqq.*
Phoenicians according to Cretan tradition improved but did not invent letters, [372], 103.
Pictographs (Cretan), in groups of 2 to 7, [300], 31.
  similar collocations of, on different stones, [301], 32.
  boustrophèdon arrangement of, [301], 32.
  personal relation of, to owner of seal, [302], 33.
  classification of, [303], 34 *seqq.*, [331], 62, [332], 63.
  Mycenaean affinities of, [317], 48 *seqq.*
  earlier classes of, [324], 55 *seqq.*
  frequency of certain types of, [300], 31.
  taken from gesture language, [300], 31.
  relation of to linear signs, [362], 93 *seqq.*
  occur on similar stones to those with linear signs, [362], 93.
  experimental reduction of, to linear forms, [363], 94.
  relation of, to Cypriote letters, [363], 94 *seqq.*
  relation of, to Semitic letters, [364], 95 *seqq.*
  relation of, to Lykian and Carian letters, 138.
Pig, pictograph, [310], 41.
Pinies, near Elunta, stone vase from, 117, 118.
Pitanê, Mycenaean vase from, [319], 50 *n.*
Plectrum, pictograph, [306], 37.
Polytechnion, Athens, Cretan seal-stones in, [276], 7, [295], 26, [297], 28.
Praesians, their traditions as to Greek settlement in Crete, [357 and *n.*], 88.
  akin to Kydonians, [357], 88.

RICHARD CLAY AND SONS, LIMITED, LONDON AND BUNGAY.

RECONSTRUCTION OF MYCENAEAN CEILING DECORATION,
FROM CRETAN GEM AND TEMPLATE SYMBOL.

For EU product safety concerns, contact us at Calle de José Abascal, 56–1°, 28003 Madrid, Spain or eugpsr@cambridge.org.

www.ingramcontent.com/pod-product-compliance
Ingram Content Group UK Ltd.
Pitfield, Milton Keynes, MK11 3LW, UK
UKHW030855150625
459647UK00021B/2795